T0085858

THE FALLING OF DUSK

THE FALLING
OF DUSK

The 2023 Lent Book

Paul Dominiak

BLOOMSBURY CONTINUUM
LONDON · OXFORD · NEW YORK · NEW DELHI · SYDNEY

BLOOMSBURY CONTINUUM
Bloomsbury Publishing Plc
50 Bedford Square, London, WC1B 3DP, UK
29 Earlsfort Terrace, Dublin 2, Ireland

BLOOMSBURY, BLOOMSBURY CONTINUUM and the Diana logo are trademarks
of Bloomsbury Publishing Plc

First published in Great Britain 2022

A catalogue record for this book is available from the British Library

Library of Congress Cataloguing-in-Publication data has been applied for

ISBN: PB: 978-1-4729-9047-1; eBook: 978-1-4729-9049-5; ePDF: 978-1-4729-9048-8

2 4 6 8 10 9 7 5 3 1

Typeset by Deanta Global Publishing Services, Chennai, India
Printed and bound in Great Britain by CPI Group (UK) Ltd, Croydon CR0 4YY

MIX
Paper | Supporting
responsible forestry
FSC® C171272

To find out more about our authors and books visit www.bloomsbury.com and
sign up for our newsletters

Dedicated to Sophia and Eleanor, my 'quiver full' of happiness
(Psalm 127.5)

Thou art all fair, my love; there is no spot in thee
(Song of Solomon 4.7)

CONTENTS

INTRODUCTION:
THE FALLING OF DUSK

As dusk falls on the end of life, a person's final words carry significant freight. This book invites you to wrestle with the meaning of Jesus's last words in the final three hours of his life as 'darkness came over the whole earth' (Mark 15.33; Matthew 27.45). Jesus speaks these words nailed to a cross from noon until his death, executed by an unholy alliance of religious and political authorities. These last words represent Christ's crucial testimony of how 'all things hold together' in him such that there is somehow 'peace through the blood of his cross' (Colossians 1.17–20).

In attending to Jesus's last words at the falling of dusk in the crucifixion, this book is both conventional and unconventional.

This book is conventional in that it follows a well-established Christian spiritual discipline of reflecting upon Jesus's last words. From as early as the second century, Christian tradition began to draw together the seven last words of Jesus on the cross recorded in the Gospels of Mark, Matthew, Luke and John. As the great North African bishop and early Christian theologian Augustine of Hippo (354–430) wrote, these last words were seen to teach Christians 'what is to be despised in this life and what is to be hoped for in eternity'.

Across the Gospels, Jesus speaks his seven last words to different people, and sometimes to God directly. The collated seven last words (or 'septenary of words on the cross') are as follows:

To God: 'Father, forgive them; for they do not know what they are doing' (Luke 23.34)

To the penitent thief: 'Truly I tell you, today you will be with me in paradise' (Luke 23.43)

To Mary, his mother: 'Woman, here is your son,' *and to the beloved disciple*: 'Here is your mother' (John 19.26–7)

To God: 'My God, my God, why have you forsaken me?' (Matthew 27.46 and Mark 15.34)

To the crowd: 'I thirst' (John 19.28)

To the world: 'It is finished' (John 19.30)

To God: 'Father, into your hands I commend my spirit' (Luke 23.46)

Medieval piety developed a devotional pedigree around these seven last words. Most often, such devotions happened as part of Lent. Lent represents an annual time of intense and intentional self-reflection in imitation of Christ's 40 days in the wilderness. The Gospels tell us that at Jesus's baptism the heavens opened, the Holy Spirit descended, and a divine voice declared him as the 'Son' and 'Beloved' with 'whom I am well pleased' (Matthew 3.13–17; Mark 1.9–11; Luke 3.21–3; compare John 1.32–3). The same Spirit immediately drove Jesus into the wilderness to be tested and refined before he begins his ministry that will culminate in the cross (Matthew 4.1–11; Mark 1.12–13; Luke 4.1–13).

Many Christians imitate Christ in the season of Lent. The Spirit 'adopts' Christians into Christ through baptism (Romans 8.15; Galatians 4.5; Ephesians 1.4). In Lent, the Spirit drives believers to undertake a yearly inward journey into a spiritual desert. Through the Lenten season, believers prepare to share in Jesus's cross-shaped ministry through spiritual practices of prayer, fasting and charity that conform them to the image and mind of Christ (Romans 8.29; Philippians 2.1–11).

Modern churches continue to practise many of the medieval devotions around the last words of Christ, even if in modified form. These devotions tend to happen in Holy Week, the final week of Lent that recapitulates the final days of Jesus's life after he 'set his face to go to Jerusalem' (Luke 9.51). Worship in Holy Week enfolds worshippers into the drama of what is known as Christ's passion – meaning his betrayal, arrest, torture and execution recorded in the Gospels. Replicating medieval practice, passion narratives are still proclaimed in worship as part of Palm Sunday and Good Friday in Holy Week. Many churches also offer the devotion known as the Stations of the Cross, which originated with the Franciscan order and became popular from the mid-fourteenth century onwards. The Stations can vary in number, but typically include readings and prayers that follow the story of Jesus's betrayal, arrest and crucifixion, including his last words. On Good Friday, the last words form the particular focus of Christian devotion as worshippers gather to commemorate the crucifixion of Christ. Many churches hold a vigil from around noon until the hour of Christ's death around 3 p.m. In doing so, they follow a popular devotional practice that began at least as early as the end of the seventeenth century in

Peru, and which soon spread across Catholic Europe. In this vigil, the gathered community meditates upon the last words of Christ on the cross. Over the course of the devotion, preachers reflect upon each last word in turn, framed by suitable poetry, music and art.

In all these devotions, the passion and last words of Christ suffuse the worship and imagination of Christians through Holy Week. The last words of Christ have inspired, then, countless Christians, writers, musicians and artists over the years to meditate upon their significance. The prevalence and diversity of ways in which Christians continue to engage with the last words of Christ testifies both to the popularity of this form of devotion and to the spiritual depth of their meaning.

This book flows as just another small tributary into a far larger devotional ocean that shapes how Christians understand themselves and God through the cross and Christ's last words. It offers a resource in which believers may immerse themselves as part of their Lenten piety. Seven chapters address seven words, one at a time. Beginning with the week of Ash Wednesday, a reader could use a chapter per week in Lent to help 'set her face to go to Jerusalem' and there discover Christ speaking on the cross.

This book is unconventional, however, in its focus. This book focuses on *doubt*. It does so for two reasons.

First, the crux of this book is that doubt broods in Jesus's last words spoken on the cross. In Latin, the word 'crux' means 'cross'. It now figuratively means something like a painful conundrum, a chief problem, or a decisive point of interest – the *crux of a matter*. This double meaning of the word captures what this book addresses. In the early sixteenth century Reformation, the German church reformer Martin Luther (1483–1546) proclaimed that 'the cross alone is our theology'. He reclaimed a biblical sense of the centrality of the cross for Christians (1 Peter 2.24–5). Our conundrum, problem and decisive interest, however, is that what we hear at the heart of the cross is a lament. The only last word on the cross repeated in more than one Gospel is Jesus's cry of dereliction: 'My God, my God, why have you forsaken me?' He speaks this word in preternatural darkness as he nears his final breath in agony. We might at first consider such doubt to be unremarkable. Ambrose of Milan (c. 339–397) – an early church bishop and saint – considered that Jesus's doubt on the cross was 'a very human response to think oneself abandoned'. While that remains true, Christians claim that Jesus is God incarnate. We cannot quite so neatly separate out Jesus's humanity and divinity as he speaks this last word so close to death. The one whom Christians recognize in the orthodox formularies of faith as being both fully human and fully divine in one person screams out that God has abandoned him. Little wonder that St Paul writes about the 'scandal of the cross' (1 Corinthians 1.17–25). At the epicentre of all the last words on the cross is a dark and violent word of doubt spoken by God to God in the face of horrendous evil. The shockwaves of this one word shudder through all seven last words that Jesus speaks. This one word shakes the sense of God's power, goodness and fidelity that underpins every other word. We cannot hear each last word isolated from the literal and figurative darkness of Christ's doubt and death as dusk falls on the cross. As we enter Jesus's seven last words, we must wrestle with the perplexing crux of the cross, rather than gloss over it.

Second, doubting God is hardly unique to Jesus. Doubting God is a decisive characteristic of our human condition with which we must all wrestle at one time or another. People of all faiths and none have doubted God throughout history. Each epoch has a right in its own way to be called an age of doubt, and not least our own. All religious doubt, however, grows from the same root of uncertainty. As soon as we talk about God, we are caught up in a dilemma of faith. 'Faith' means to put trust in something or someone we perceive to be trustworthy. Doubt is logically dependent upon faith. It is uncertain belief in the trustworthiness of the object of faith. The author of the Epistle to the Hebrews defines the theological virtue of 'faith' as 'the assurance of things hoped for, the conviction of things not seen' (Hebrews 11.1). The definition captures the dilemma of faith: how can we steadfastly trust that which we cannot see? For Christians, God is inherently trustworthy and certain because God is perfect. 'I am the Lord,' we hear in the Scriptures, 'and I do not change' (Malachi 3.6). We are exhorted to trust or have faith in God's fidelity. 'Trust in the Lord forever,' we are exhorted, 'for in the Lord God you have an everlasting rock' (Isaiah 26.4). Yet, God's perfection remains above and beyond all of creation and human knowing. As St Paul puts it, God 'dwells in unapproachable light, whom no one has ever seen or can see' (1 Timothy 6.6). Elsewhere, St Paul writes that, even as we taste the sweetness of God in this life, 'for now we see in a mirror, darkly' (1 Corinthians 13.12). A gap exists between our experience of God's faithfulness and God's transcendence that exceeds our ability to comprehend. The most intrinsically certain God is also the most unknowable to our ordinary ways of knowing. In this gap, the world as we experience it can both confirm and deny God's goodness, power and presence. We struggle to make sense of God in the vicissitudes and messiness of life. We doubt.

This gap is the falling of dusk on unabashed certainty. Doubt looms in the penumbra between knowledge and ignorance. Doubt attends all experiences of faith. None of us can slip out of our own skin. Neither can we escape the incommensurability between our creaturely finitude and the radical otherness of God. If God really is who and what Christians claim, then all our words necessarily fail. Language falls short of adequately capturing God. We have totally valid questions that are always going to be utterly unanswerable in any final sense. This is the wound of knowledge in all theological talk. As the Welsh metaphysical poet Henry Vaughan (1621–1695) wrote, 'there is in God, some say, / A deep but dazzling darkness.' Doubt is the condition of humanity, limited as we are, being capable only of a restricted view, not least of a transcendent God.

In this universal condition of doubt, some believe too much and others too little, to paraphrase the English literary critic Terry Eagleton (b. 1943). We might understandably run away from doubt to protect our faith, seeing doubt as a threat or as a moral weakness. Doubt threatens, after all, to leave the believer insecure in faith and uncertain in life. The Epistle of James evocatively images this danger: 'one who doubts is like a wave of the sea that is driven and tossed about by the wind' (James 1.6). Far better to let an uncritical faith take hold than risk losing it, we might think. Alternatively, we might embrace doubt too tightly and begin to deny God even exists. Here, we might see faith as the enemy of reasonable doubt and honest enquiry. Doubt, we might think, allows us to question and face reality. Radical doubt on this account liberates us from immaturity and illusion. It cures us of religion and its sacred myths. At their respective extremes, too much faith and too much doubt slide into dogmatic rigidity. When intractable dogmatism of any kind becomes wedded to politics, it can kill, as history and our contemporary world shows.

This book joins together these two fallings of dusk – Jesus's doubt on the cross, and our common human experience of doubt. This knitting of Jesus's last words and our human condition holds much promise as we meditate upon them together. The falling of dusk on the cross heralds both the withering away of uncritical certitude and the promised dawn of a chastened way of apprehending the intelligibility of God. When we attend to the doubt that beats in the heart of the cross, we can feel the pulse of our human doubt being taken in the heart of God. Rather than seeing doubt as contrary to faith – and vice versa – we might be able to begin to see them as integral to human understanding. Doubt and certainty meet in Christ, who is fully human and yet also fully God. This union of natures in Christ describes what the Christian faith calls 'incarnation'. The incarnation is the gift of God's self-emptying in Christ (Philippians 2.1–11). Christ enfolds the entirety of human nature into the heart of God. 'The Word became flesh and lived among us,' the Gospel of John records, and 'to all who received him, who believed in his name, he gave power to become children of God' (John 1.12, 14). A popular patristic maxim captured this scriptural idea of a miraculous exchange in Christ's incarnation. Irenaeus (c. 130–202) wrote, for example, that Christ 'become what we are, that He might bring us to be even what He is Himself'. In other words, Christ translates human finitude into God's transcendence, and the other way around. The divine embrace of human nature in the incarnation includes our limit and doubt, taking it into the certain faithfulness of God. Such grace continually disrupts our ways of being, knowing and doing as we share in Christ. As Christ graces our human nature, he lends a certain kind of grace to doubt.

This book explores, then, how religious conviction remains possible even without certainty, and how faith and doubt necessarily co-exist. It shows how we might chart a middle course between the two extremes relating to doubt, namely religious dogmatism and doctrinaire atheism. Each of these extremes in their own way foreclose openness to the disruptive grace of the crucified one who claims to be 'the way, the truth, and the life' (John 14.6).

As each chapter in this book meditates, then, on one of the seven last words of Christ, they do so in conversation with some of the great doubters of Christianity and religion in the modern world. Some readers may find the atheism of the conversation partners surprising as part of a devotional practice. These conversation partners include the 'masters of suspicion' of the nineteenth and early twentieth centuries, modern New Atheists, and philosophers who think Christianity cannot reconcile suffering with God's goodness and omnipotence. Other readers may be surprised to discover theological voices from the Christian tradition that advocate a certain kind of 'theological atheism' within Christianity. By drawing upon an apparent cacophony of voices, this book seeks to conduct a more polyphonic harmony. Too often, atheists dismiss religions as mad, bad, sad and dangerous to know. In turn, Christians too readily dismiss atheist arguments against religious belief as reductive, misleading and beside the point. Instead of a conversation, we hear only echo chambers and monologues. The East German Marxist philosopher Ernst Bloch (1885–1977) once provocatively observed that 'only an atheist can be a good Christian; only a Christian can be a good atheist'. This book plays with that idea to take seriously the radical claims of faith and doubt as mutually refining. Everyone is welcome to this conversation. Everyone is respected. While the author of this book is a professing Christian, this is not a book exclusively for Christians alone. It is also for those who might be suspicious about faith, but whose doubt might lead them into new and unexpected vistas after all.

This journey of faithful doubt remains suited for the season of Lent as it leads to the cross. In the wilderness of Lent, all is stripped and bleached bare. In this spiritual wilderness, there is no hiding from the fiercely antiseptic sun of arid day, or from the lonely chill of wintry night. Exposing faith to doubt and darkness tests and refines it into something stronger, like tempered steel. Exposing doubt to the faith of the cross transfigures it into part of the way in which God unfolds and unfurls in the frailty of human nature, all of which is held up on the cross. Jesus doubts on that cross. There is much we might doubt in the claims he makes in his last words too. To doubt is not faithless. Rather, to doubt means to share faithfully in the whole reality of Christ as he encircles the fullness of our humanity. It is to enter the falling of dusk and wrestle with what we hear there. This booked extends an invitation, then, not merely to those who profess to be Christian. It invites everyone to struggle honestly with doubt, faith and what it means to be human.

I

'FORGIVE'

When they came to the place that is called The Skull, they crucified Jesus there with the criminals, one on his right and one on his left. Then Jesus said, 'Father, forgive them; for they do not know what they are doing.'

Luke 23.33–4

There was really only one Christian, and he died on the cross.

Friedrich Nietzsche (1844–1900)

I don't have a minute to hate, I'm gonna pursue justice for the rest of my life.

Mamie Till-Mobley (1921–2003)

If anyone knows anything about Christianity, it is the critical role accorded to forgiveness in the teachings and practices of Jesus. When Jesus teaches his disciples to pray, he includes as part of the Lord's Prayer the petition 'forgive us our debts as we have also forgiven our debtors' (Mark 6.9–13), which Luke alternatively records as 'forgive us our sins, for we ourselves forgive everyone indebted to us' (Luke 11.2–4). Jesus repeats the reciprocity between forgiving others and being forgiven by God at numerous other points (Mark 11.25; Matthew 6.14–15; Luke 6.37; John 20.23). Jesus says that it is not enough simply to forgive someone seven times, but seventy-seven times (Matthew 18.21–2), which implies as often as is needed. Jesus walks the talk of forgiveness too. He forgives the woman caught in adultery when others are ready to kill her (John 8.11). He forgives the sins of those who come to him for healing (Mark 2.5; Matthew 9.2). He forgives Peter's triple denial of him in the crucifixion narrative, restoring him to discipleship (John 21.17). Forgiveness shapes the whole of Christ's life, death and resurrection. 'In him,' St Paul writes, 'we have redemption through his blood, the forgiveness of our trespasses, according to the riches of his grace' (Ephesians 1.7). And now, in his first last word, Jesus prays to the Father to forgive the litany of people involved in his brutal torture and murder: 'Father, forgive them; for they do not know what they are doing' (Luke 23.34).

What is happening when Jesus prays this first last word? The word 'forgiveness' derives from an Old English word that means something like 'to pardon an offence' or 'to give up the power to punish'. The New Testament has four main Greek words to describe forgiveness: the verbs 'aphiemi', 'charizomai' and 'apoluo'; and the noun 'aphesis'. These four main words have a similar meaning to the Old English root of the word 'forgiveness'. They describe the remission, pardon or cancellation of a debt or punishment, as well as setting someone free from a burden. In the New Testament, forgiving someone does not undo the event of wrongdoing. Rather, forgiveness pardons the *guilt* and *punishment* that results from such an event. Whether in its Greek or Old English etymology, to forgive means to relinquish the power to punish. It displays the contrary power to set someone free. It frees the wrongdoer from guilt. It also frees the victim from hate.

Forgiving and being forgiven are risky business. As Rowan Williams writes, 'the person who asks forgiveness has renounced the privilege of being right or safe' and 'the person who forgives has renounced the safety of being locked into the position of the offended victim'. As such, 'both the giver and the receiver of forgiveness have moved out of the safety zone; they have begun to ask how to receive their humanity as a gift'. Forgiveness involves the giver and recipient losing full control and power. It promises an alternative but unpredictable interpersonal power that depends upon the giver and receiver rediscovering one another in vulnerability. The interpersonal power of forgiveness can resurrect a broken relationship for an unknown future of new possibilities. It helps us discover what it means to be human in the messiness of life.

At his most powerless – beaten to a pulp, nearly naked, nailed to a cross – Jesus shows his power paradoxically by giving up the power to punish. In this first last word, he withholds hatred or vengeance. Jesus would have been justified to seek justice rather than mercy. The law of retribution in the Old Testament is clear about the equitable principle of exact retaliation for wrongdoing.

The ordinances in Exodus say, 'if any harm follows [from someone's actions], then you shall give life for life, eye for eye, tooth for tooth, hand for hand, foot for foot, burn for burn, wound for wound, stripe for stripe' (Exodus 21.24–5). Repeating this sentiment, Deuteronomy is brutally clear that judges should 'show no pity' to false witnesses, taking 'life for life, eye for eye' (Deuteronomy 19.21). Instead, Jesus prays for his heavenly Father to forgive those who falsely witness against him, those who bay for his blood, and those who execute him. He prays for forgiveness even as they callously mock him and 'cast lots to divide his clothing' (Luke 23.34–8), showing themselves incapable of receiving his first last word for 'they do not know what they are doing' (Luke 23.34). On the cross, Jesus embodies his teaching in the Sermon on the Mount about non-retribution. 'You have heard,' Jesus preaches, 'that it was said, "An eye for an eye and a tooth for a tooth." But I say to you, Do not resist an evildoer. But if anyone strikes you on the right cheek, turn the other also' (Matthew 5.38–9). 'Love your enemies,' he continues, 'and pray for those who persecute you, so that you may be children of your Father in heaven' (Matthew 5.44–5). 'Be perfect,' Jesus then exhorts, 'as your heavenly Father is perfect' (Matthew 5.48). Now, as he dies, Jesus's first last word of forgiveness embodies the desire to see right relationships restored and an endless cycle of violence interrupted. It is a word of love. It incarnates the perfection of God accommodated to human frailty. It disrupts our ordinary ways with the risk of grace and the possibility of a new way of seeing the world and one another.

As anyone who has tried it knows, forgiveness is easy to say and hard to do. It feels unnatural in a way the law of retribution does not. Forgiveness sometimes involves more personal cost than the offence suffered in the first place. It involves giving up power when you already feel powerless and vulnerable. The Gospel of Luke rarely gives us psychological insight into what Jesus feels. If anything, Luke's Jesus maintains philosophic composure as he is crucified. Yet, this first last word in the terrible vulnerability of the cross must have *hurt* to say and mean. The Gospels do not dwell on specific horrors in the torture and murder of Christ. The brutal realities of crucifixions were well known to Jews and Gentiles alike living within Roman imperial rule. We are unfamiliar, however, with crucifixions. We rely on simulacra in art and film. Whatever crucified horrors they depict, we nevertheless know they are not real themselves.

It is therefore perhaps easy to gloss over the horrendous evils Jesus undergoes in his passion. To do so risks losing the intense *cost* of the forgiveness he prays for in this first last word. In the ancient Roman world, crucifixion was designed to humiliate, degrade and dehumanize the victim. Crucifixions were reserved for the worst sort of criminals, such as those crucified either side of Jesus. As Fleming Rutledge puts it, crucifixion 'was a form of advertisement, or public announcement – this person is the scum of the earth, not fit to live, more an insect than a human being.' Innocent though he is, Jesus is 'counted among the lawless' and brutally murdered on the cross, pouring 'out his life unto death' (Luke 22.37; cf. Isaiah 53.12).

The early theologian Origen (184–253) emphasized 'the utterly vile death of the cross'. It was vile. Crucifixions ritualized physical and psychological forms of public torture. They often involved sexual degradation. We see all these elements in what the Gospels record about the passion of Christ. He was stripped naked before being brutally scourged. He was mocked without mercy in word and deed. The Roman soldiers brutalized and spat upon his body. They dressed him with a crown of thorns, a purple robe and a mock sceptre to parody the claims he is a king. Crippled, Jesus was unable to bear the weight of the cross on the journey of sorrows to Golgotha, the Place of the Skull. A baying crowd heaped abuse upon him as he died. He was roughly tied to a cross, nails piercing his flesh. The crowds and brigands executed with Jesus continued to ridicule him in his utter helplessness. Crucifixions caused intense agony and bodily shame. The weight of the crucified body disrupted normal breathing, making exhalation nearly impossible as time went on. Bodily functions went unchecked. A crucifixion sought to break a transgressor in body and spirit, as well as dissuade anyone else from dissent or disregard of authority and law. As Fleming Rutledge points out, in Jesus's crucifixion, 'all the evil impulses of the human race came to focus in him'.

We cannot overstate the vulgarity of the cross, not only physically but in theological terms too. As Dietrich Bonhoeffer (1906–1945) wrote, 'God lets himself be pushed out of the world on to the cross'. In the crucifixion, Jesus is stripped of his humanity and his divinity denied. Crucifixion *hurts* Jesus psychologically as much as physically. The Romans described people they crucified as 'condemned to the death of a beast'. The Roman statesman Cicero called crucifixion 'that plague'. Crucifixion was equally abhorrent to Jewish imaginations. The Jewish historian Josephus described crucifixion as 'the most wretched of deaths'. In the Old Testament, a divine curse was seen to hang over anyone who had committed a crime punishable by death (Deuteronomy 21.22–3; cf. Deuteronomy 31.23). Christ on the cross accordingly became a 'curse for us' (Galatians 3.13). As such, St Paul recognized the violence of the cross as a 'scandal' or 'stumbling block' to belief, whether one was a Gentile or a Jew (Galatians 5.11). It was obscene and absurd to think that the accursed scum of the earth could in any way save anyone. Early Christians endured ridicule as a result. An early third-century piece of Roman graffiti, for example, shows a man praying to a stupid ass nailed to a cross. Underneath, a scrawled inscription in Greek reads, 'Alexamenos worships his god.'

In this first last word, however, we see how Jesus 'for the sake of the joy that was set before him endured the cross, disregarding its shame' (Hebrews 12.2). 'For the message about the cross is foolishness to those who are perishing,' wrote St Paul, 'but to us who are being saved it is the power of God' (1 Corinthians 1.18). In Christ, we see the exemplar of divine love as it disrupts the evil of which we are capable. Nevertheless, the catalogue of cruelty in Jesus's final hours on the cross means that praying for forgiveness must have *cost* him. It must have *hurt* just as much as being broken in body and spirit as he is stripped, whipped, mocked and nailed – all the while praying for forgiveness. This is the 'mind of Christ' (1 Corinthians 2.16) which Christians are called to proclaim and imitate. Like a broken body awaiting resurrection, forgiveness is 'sown in weakness' but 'raised in power' (1 Corinthians 15.43).

Not everyone is always convinced that Christians are any better than the rest of the population at following the forgiveness practised by Jesus. They have every right to be suspicious. It is easy to pay lip service to forgiveness. It is harder to engage with forgiveness in its emotional complexity. We all recognize the cost of forgiveness in our own lives. We all shy away from it. Little wonder that Christians are often more known for judgement and exclusion than for forgiveness and loving embrace. 'I like your Christ, I do not like your Christians,' as Mahatma Gandhi reputedly said. 'You Christians are so unlike your Christ,' he then purportedly averred. This apocryphal comment stands well as a cipher for popular sentiments about Christians. Centuries of dogmatism, prejudice and hate committed by Christians give power to Alfred Loisy's (1857–1940) biting remark that 'Jesus foretold the Kingdom, and it was the Church that came.'

Friedrich Nietzsche saw the hypocrisy that often marks Christianity's claim to be a religion of love and forgiveness. He was one of what the French philosopher Paul Ricoeur (1913–2005) called the 'great masters of suspicion' of religion. 'There was really only one Christian,' Nietzsche wrote, 'and he died on the cross.' By contrast, 'the Christians have never practised the actions Jesus prescribed them'. For

Nietzsche, Christians talked about Christ in the abstract terms of faith but failed to follow his ways. As we will see, he did not simply think this was an effect of human frailty. Something altogether more suspicious was at play in Christianity. What he uncovered, he thought, rendered the Christian idea of forgiveness as a masquerade for something far more sinister. What he found asks us to question what lurks in our hearts as we meditate upon this first last word about forgiveness. His doubt makes us honest. We must engage with him as we face this first last word.

Nietzsche became infamous for his militant atheism, for proclaiming that 'God is dead' and for his eventual descent into madness and death, probably caused by neuro-syphilis. His life began as one immersed in faith, however, even if by adulthood it became shaped by intense doubt. Nietzsche was born in 1844 in Prussia, the son and grandson of Lutheran clergymen. Both of his parents embraced Pietist revivalism with its emphasis on religious enthusiasm, a personal relationship with Christ, and living a sanctified life. At one time, Nietzsche hoped to follow in the clerical footsteps of his father and grandfathers. From an early age he certainly imbibed his parents' religious sensibility. As a child, Nietzsche was mocked by his peers as the 'little pastor', so deep was his piety. Yet, within a term of studying theology at university, he lost his faith. Among his reasons for losing faith, Nietzsche had read Ludwig Feuerbach's (1804–1872) *The Essence of Christianity*, published in 1841. A radical German philosopher, Feuerbach argued that the people had created God, and not the other way around. Theology was human nature projected upwards.

To explain the origin of religion, then, we had to uncover its actual human foundations, the 'true or anthropological essence of religion'. In other words, one had to *suspect* the supernatural claims that religion made and explain them in a way that was true to material reality. For Feuerbach, religion represented the projection of the needs and desires of human consciousness. Similarly, following Feuerbach, what Andrew Cole calls Nietzsche's 'suspicious explanations' unearthed truths that Nietzsche thought religion had hidden. In fact, Christianity had distorted how everyone perceived reality. As such, it inhibited true human flourishing. Nietzsche's whole philosophical project aimed to save the soul of society from what he began to see as the diseased imagination of Christianity.

Nietzsche took aim at what he called the 'slave morality' of Christianity. He excavated the origins of 'slave morality' in his work *On the Genealogy of Morality*, published in 1887. As Nietzsche saw it, far from being fixed and eternal, what we took as 'good' and 'evil' were conventions. We might better phrase them as *inventions*, for Christianity had inverted the actual conditions for human flourishing, reifying weakness over strength. This 'revolt...has two thousand years of history behind it,' wrote Nietzsche, 'and which has only been lost sight of because – it was victorious.' Nietzsche sought to lift the veil on Christianity and its distortion of human potential. Christian claims about love and forgiveness were a sham.

To explore how this was the case, Nietzsche invited his readers in the *Genealogy* to imagine a society composed of masters and slaves.

As he imagined them, 'masters' are powerful, active and healthy. 'Goodness' here merely describes the conditions for human flourishing. Nietzsche framed 'master morality' as a sort of equation where 'good = noble = powerful = beautiful = happy = blessed'. When masters suffer grievance, they immediately discharge a proportionate and retributive response that allows them to get on with their lives. Forgiveness does not feature within their emotional ecology, except as an act of magnanimity. Nietzsche had in mind ancient Greco-Roman cultures as historical examples of this imagined 'master morality'.

For Nietzsche, 'badness' in turn originally described the contrary conditions that inhibit human flourishing. In his imagined society, those who are incapable of leading a 'good' life – most notably the 'slaves', 'herd' or 'plebeians' – are 'bad' only insofar as they cannot live the exuberant kind of life that the 'masters' do. Faced with their impotence, and unable to take physical revenge upon their masters, 'slaves' develop a negative sentiment that Nietzsche called 'ressentiment.' This French word describes an intense hostility emerging from suppressed feelings of envy and hatred that cannot be discharged physically because the slaves lack power.

Yet, this 'ressentiment' turns creative, Nietzsche argued. The slaves take *psychological* revenge on their masters. The slaves invent a new concept, namely that of 'evil'. 'Slave morality' is born, and it is a twisted inversion of master morality. 'Evil' describes the masters – those who live flourishing lives. 'Evil' takes on a moral value as something to judge and which needs forgiveness. In turn, the slaves imagine 'goodness' to be their own condition, even though it is the antithesis of human flourishing. The deleterious condition the slaves live under bizarrely become something morally praiseworthy.

Nietzsche located the historical eruption of this imaginary 'slave morality' in the Jewish and Christian religions. The 'unfathomable…hatred of the powerless', Nietzsche wrote, referring to the Judaeo-Christian tradition, '[says] only those who suffer are good, only the poor, the powerless, the lowly are good; the suffering, the deprived, the sick, the ugly, are the only pious people, the only ones saved.' At the same time, the Judaeo-Christian morality proclaims 'whereas you rich, the noble and powerful, you are eternally wretched, cursed and damned!' While the Judaeo-Christian tradition speaks about love, Nietzsche thought, such 'love grew out of hatred, as its crown'. To illustrate how such hatred wears a mask of love, Nietzsche quotes with relish from the Christian theologians Thomas Aquinas and Tertullian, both of whom speak of how the 'blessed' rejoice at the miseries and tortures of the damned. The 'horrible paradox' of a 'God on the Cross' for Nietzsche represented a 'dangerous bait' to intoxicate minds with the language of forgiveness and render them unable to see clearly. Christianity was born out of hatred of the powerful. It only wears the garment of love as a smokescreen. Christian morality had rendered society weak, insipid and incapable of reaching its 'highest potential power and splendour'. Nietzsche poured his invective over Christianity as a result. He vented that, 'I condemn Christianity…I call Christianity the one great curse, the one great innermost corruption, the one great instinct for revenge...[,] the one immortal blot on humanity.'

Giles Fraser in *Redeeming Nietzsche* (2002) argues that Nietzsche's work offered, in effect, an alternative salvation story to Christianity, 'a form of redemption that would work for a post-theistic age'. Nietzsche's adult suspicions led him to doubt the truth of Christianity. His suspicion held explanatory power, he thought, not just for him but for everyone. It allowed people to view the world properly. It redeemed people from the false, pathological and repressive teachings of Christianity. It freed them for truth and human creativity. What this might look like was up to the reader once they have been freed.

Whatever we make of Nietzsche's overall argument, Giles Fraser reminds us that, in one regard at least, Nietzsche remains psychologically perceptive. *Forgiveness* and *anger* are inextricably bound together. We do not simply *forget* when we forgive. Residual pain and anger remain. So too can the desire linger in the human heart to punish or take revenge, even as we resist that violence in forgiveness. Fraser explains how 'the non-violent resistance of evil often has for those who seek to practise it the psychological consequence of intensifying and magnifying feelings of hostility towards the "evil" they resist, and Christians are often insufficiently honest about this.' He then explains this phenomenon in blunter terms. 'I may respond to your striking me by turning the other cheek,' Fraser writes, 'but in my guts I still want to punch you back'. What Nietzsche calls 'ressentiment' – the frustrated condition of hostility

– attends any act of forgiveness. When we forgive, we divest the power to punish. We feel powerless, just as we did when we suffered at someone else's hands in the first place. We have not discharged the hatred that desires to lash back and get even. We are vulnerable. We hurt. We bear anger, even hatred, in our hearts. Nietzsche makes us be *honest* about what we *feel*, even as we forgive.

Yet, Jesus's first last word on the cross shows that Nietzsche gets the link between 'ressentiment' and forgiveness in the wrong order. What we experience when we forgive – this 'ressentiment' – is 'the child of Christianity', as the French philosopher René Girard (1923–2015) put it, but not its 'father'. Rather, as Girard continues, 'the Bible and the Gospels have diminished the violence of vengeance and turned it to *ressentiment*…because their real target is vengeance in all its forms, and they have succeeded in wounding vengeance, not eliminating it.' Christ's first last word shows how forgiveness interrupts the cycle of violence and shame. Forgiveness disrupts vengeance.

For Girard (and Giles Fraser, who turns to him), Nietzsche fails to confront the brutal realities of human vengeance. In the cross, however, we see its visceral reality before us. An unholy alliance of religion and politics executes an innocent man before an unruly mob baying for blood. Vengeance is certainly deserved. Yet, to do so would only legitimate and feed the vicious human economy of retribution and its endless cycle of violence. 'You hurt me, and I hurt you back' is the logic of retaliation – and its effects are monstrous, not fleeting or ephemeral. The reality of vengeance burns like a fire, consuming lives throughout history. The violence endemic to human society conflagrates beyond the view of the cross – but the cross allows us to see it squarely in all its horror and futility.

Christ's first last word – 'Father, forgive them' – invites God to speak something new into this human society. It invites God to divest the power to punish and open a new vista where relationships based on peace might be recreated. 'I am about to do a new thing,' the Lord says to the prophet Isaiah, 'now it springs forth, do you not perceive it?' (Isaiah 43.19). In Christ's first last word, we see this new thing, 'a way in the wilderness and rivers in the desert'. A new thing is the way and word of the cross.

'See, I am making all things new,' Christ says in a heavenly vision to John of Patmos (Revelation 21.5). The eruption of divine forgiveness in Christ's first last word on the cross is the making all things new. Forgiveness is the beginning – but certainly not the end – of restoring right relations, which is really what 'righteousness' means. Forgiveness eschews violence by exposing its brutality and infertility on the cross. It reveals a different, divine way.

None of this denies the emotional cost of the residual anger, resentment and pain that lingers even as we forgive. We all know to our cost that we have been hurt and that we have hurt others. We can *forgive*, but not *forget*. This lingering 'ressentiment' reflects, however, what René Girard called the 'interiorization of weakened vengeance'. It's the afterbirth of forgiveness, the 'manner in which the spirit of vengeance survives the impact of Christianity'. It is the emotional cost we are left to deal with as we forgive – and it is a far lesser evil than the terrifying and endless violence of vengeance. In fact, it is the shadow of an immense, possible good. Forgiveness opens the door to reconciliation, whether within us, with others, or with God. It paves the way towards the peace for which we were made. It is why Christians proclaim that 'Christ is our peace', for in this first last word that is what he speaks to us. Peace is a cross-shaped word.

In his first last word, Jesus confronts us to be honest about the liberating potential and hard challenge of forgiveness. If we are dishonest about what we feel as we forgive – and what forgiveness demands of the giver and receiver – we run the risk of what Dietrich Bonhoeffer called 'cheap grace'. By this, Bonhoeffer meant 'grace without discipleship, grace without the cross, grace without Jesus Christ, living and incarnate'. To forgive is costly. It requires us to divest power and trust in another who has shown themselves capable of hurting us. It is a leap of faith in the hope of healing, for oneself and for another.

To take being forgiven seriously is costly too. To be forgiven requires a change of heart, or what the New Testament calls *repentance*. The Greek word for repentance, 'metanoia', denotes a radical reorientation of perspective, a change of mind about oneself, others and God. When we repent, we do not flinch from seeing the harm we have done and who that suggests we are. We take the risk of asking someone else to bestow a new humanity on us and restore a right relationship. We realize we depend upon someone else for our freedom, and we share in the vulnerability and hurt we caused them.

Both the giver and receiver of forgiveness become a *new thing*. Forgiveness is the beginning – but certainly not the end – of the hard work of being fully human. Forgiveness restores relationships between human beings but also between humanity and God (Luke 24.47; Acts 2.39, 5.31, 10.43, 13.38, 26.18). It is costly – but God through Christ on the cross shares in that cost and reveals its divine potential.

Nietzsche keeps us *honest* as we hear this first last word of Christ. We are called to be suspicious of what is going on in our hearts as we forgive or are forgiven. We are called to judicious realism that we must take seriously the hard and complex work of reconciliation begun in forgiveness. Anger has an understandable place in the emotional ecology of forgiveness. It needs to be refined by the theological virtues of faith, hope and love. Otherwise, anger can revert to hatred and revenge, reigniting the violence that mars and distorts human lives.

'For they do not know what they do,' Jesus says as he prays for the Father to forgive. It seems a strange thing to say, for those who torture and kill him are sentient beings who consciously commit their acts of atrocity. As he speaks this first last word, however, Jesus clings onto the faith, hope and love that human beings are intrinsically *good*. As a Jew, Jesus knows that human beings are made in the image and likeness of God (Genesis 1.27). Along with all of creation, God declares them as 'good'. We are naturally oriented to goodness, meaning that which gives life. God is goodness itself, of course, and so we are all naturally oriented towards

God as our supreme good. Evil has no existence of its own. It is not part of the created order willed by God. It is the absence of good, or what the ancients called the 'privation of goodness'. We experience that absence as pain and horror – and it is the opposite of what God intends for the creation he loves. It is the failure of our *good* nature. We cannot desire evil as evil. If we choose evil – and we all do, in our own ways – it is the failure to recognize it as evil, and even perversely to misapprehend it as good. 'They do not know what they do' – this does not deny moral culpability or the unimaginable evils that people commit. It simply denies that this is the definitive *last* word about anybody. In saying 'they do not know what they do', Jesus keeps the door open for forgiveness to disrupt, reorient and transform creation, making all things new.

We sorely need to wrestle with forgiveness. We live in an angry age. People have a right to be angry, of course. Women are angry as centuries of patriarchy have oppressed them, and the way it still objectifies their bodies, denies them equal access to opportunity, and quite literally abuses and even kills them. People of colour are angry as they continue to struggle in the racist shadows of white colonial history. Poor people are angry that they are getting poorer while the few enjoy wealth beyond imagining or necessity. Others – and most notably the young – are angry as the marriage of hyper-capitalism and geopolitics wrecks the planet and devastates our ecological future for short-term gains. The global coronavirus pandemic has unveiled how all these hurts are interconnected in intricate and invidious ways, with the impact falling most heavily upon the poor, women and people of colour. It comes as little surprise that division, distrust, anxiety and mutual suspicion are the headlines of our political lives together today. It comes as even less surprise that hatred and violence often erupt.

There is no grand solution to all these evils. We can only start with the risk of speaking small words of forgiveness, spoken to those around us. We can take the residual emotional cost of forgiveness as we try to make amends with them. That doesn't mean we should not challenge or expect change, or to be challenged and changed ourselves. 'Repentance and forgiveness of sins' are both pre-conditions for reconciliation (Luke 24.47). We are called to bear the *cost* of anger in the hope for something new. We cannot shortcut this anger. Indeed, it may be that the anger we feel as we forgive can be just and must be faced. After all, the offer of forgiveness makes a demand for total conversion on the recipient and giver alike. That begins with the painful reckoning with the injury committed. If neither party faces up to the hurt experienced and anger still felt in forgiveness, neither person will ever be fully free. A relationship will never be totally restored. Unresolved anger easily grows like a tumour into hatred. As the cross shows, hatred is futile, but all too human a temptation.

Nietzsche shows us that we cannot circumvent anger. It is an intrinsic part of forgiveness. If we do not face up to the anger that remains in forgiveness, it will 'not produce God's righteousness' (James 1.20). We short circuit the emotional complexity of forgiveness if we avoid the anger still felt. As such, we restrict the capacity of forgiveness to transform both the giver and recipient of forgiveness as they face that anger in faith, hope and love.

Anger can have a divine quality to it within the way of forgiveness. The Scriptures tell us that 'the Lord is slow to anger' (Numbers 14.18; Nehemiah 9.17; Psalm 103.8, 145.8; Joel 2.13). God nevertheless still exhibits *righteous* anger against *injustice*. Jesus does the same in his ministry (Mark 3.5). The seed of forgiveness demands complete conversion for reconciliation to flower. The risk taken in forgiveness is for that purpose and end. We take the cost of residual anger to create a new thing. 'Those with good sense are slow to anger,' says Proverbs, 'and it is their glory to overlook an offense' (Proverbs 19.11). The glory described here is 'a human being fully alive', as Irenaeus memorably put it. The 'fully alive' person that Irenaeus has in mind is Jesus Christ. The fullness of human life 'is the vision of God', Irenaeus explains. What we see and hear in Jesus and his first last word is the divine fullness of right relations that forgiveness heralds. It demands risk-taking and vulnerability. It does not guarantee success. It promises resurrection and the bestowing of a new humanity. Forgiveness does not mean the giver and recipient ignore anger. It means they reckon and wrestle with it. To fail to do so threatens not taking forgiveness seriously enough, to render it as cheap grace that does not take deep hold as a new reality in the giver or recipient. Forgiveness is not forgetting. It is transformation. It rejects the violence of hate, not the justice of anger.

What all of this looks like will take on myriad guises in our lives and communities. Jesus's first last word shows that we can't hate our way through hurt without becoming trapped by it. To be fully alive, to be fully human, means seeing the vision of God in one another through the lens of the cross. Forgiveness describes that dynamic in action. It costs us. It saves us. It implicates us in questions of righteousness and justice. Forgiveness flowers as we answer these questions.

The Hebraic and Greek words we translate as 'righteousness' refer less to moral integrity than they do to the setting right of relations. 'Righteousness' is a dynamic action rather than an abstract state of being. In the Scriptures, 'justice' closely aligns with 'righteousness'. Scriptural 'justice' does not revolve around punishment. Rather, 'justice' describes the conditions that permit right relationships to be re-established. Justice is the full reckoning by both the giver and recipient of forgiveness with what has happened. It looks for loving restitution as a free response that flows out of the total conversion of the wrongdoer. Justice conditions how a new thing – the righting of relations – can be possible. It conditions how the promise of forgiveness can flower into the fullness of human beings fully alive in right relations with one another. It is our sharing in the character of God revealed to us on the cross.

The South African theologian, activist, and artist Mpho Tutu van Furth (b. 1963) writes of how the repairing of relationships, 'begins with a posture' – namely, that of 'humility' and 'love'. Humility opens us up to saying sorry for the evils we have committed as a prelude to the repairing of relationships. Love returns the humanity of the victim and perpetrator alike. It seeks wholeness. For Mpho Tutu van Furth, the repairing of relationships is like a dance that draws together earnest repentance, just reparations, and free forgiveness as a complex dance moving towards relational wholeness. 'Remorseful apology and reparation twined with gracious forgiveness', she writes, '[are] strands of hope woven together to make a better future than the one promised to us'. Repairing relationships is a dance that comprehends the emotional complexity that reconciliation entails. It reckons with anger as part of the healing journey.

'Righteousness and justice are the foundation of your throne,' the psalmist declares of God, 'steadfast love and faithfulness go before you' (Psalm 89.14). 'To do righteousness and justice is more acceptable to the Lord than sacrifice,' we hear in Proverbs (Proverbs 21.3). 'Let justice roll down like waters,' says the prophet Amos, 'and righteousness like an ever-flowing stream' (Amos 5.24). Forgiveness – and the anger that resides within it – can change the giver and recipient alike. As part of the setting right of relations, anger can have a place in the ecology of forgiveness, righteousness and justice. We must reckon with anger, or it consumes us and forgiveness withers on the vine. 'Be angry but do not sin,' says St Paul, 'do not let the sun go down on your anger' (Ephesians 4.26).

Perhaps the best *last* word for this chapter belongs, then, to Mamie Till-Mobley. Mamie was Emmett Till's mother. Emmett was a 14-year-old African American boy who was murdered in 1955 after allegedly flirting with a white woman. He was abducted by racist white vigilantes, beaten until they took one of his eyes out, shot through the head, and dumped in a river. His body was found several days later.

Despite pressure from the US government, Mamie decided to have an open casket funeral for Emmett. As she stood at the pulpit, looking down at her son's mangled body, she said to mourners, 'I don't have a minute to hate, I'm gonna pursue justice for the rest of my life.'

Mamie embraced a vocation of civil rights advocacy, starting with seeking justice for the death of her son. Forgiveness rejects hatred but does not circumvent anger and justice. Murderous white supremacy could not be simply declared forgiven without encountering anger. It had to be transformed through the actual complexity of deep forgiveness. Anger and justice had to be known and understood. It was the precondition for the complete conversion of racism. It was how the power of forgiveness to free both the giver and recipient would work in order that there might be racial reconciliation.

The challenge of Jesus's first last word about forgiveness is how willing we are to embrace Mamie Till-Mobley's rejection of hate and pursuit of justice in our own lives.

2

'BE'

One of the criminals who were hanged there kept deriding him and saying, 'Are you not the Messiah? Save yourself and us!' But the other rebuked him, saying, 'Do you not fear God, since you are under the same sentence of condemnation? And we indeed have been condemned justly, for we are getting what we deserve for our deeds, but this man has done nothing wrong.' Then he said, 'Jesus, remember me when you come into your kingdom.' He replied, 'Truly I tell you, today you will be with me in Paradise.'

Luke 23.39–42

Religion is the sigh of the oppressed creature, the heart of a heartless world, and the soul of soulless conditions. It is the opium of the people.

Karl Marx (1818–1883)

When the present is limiting – oppressive – one looks to the future for a reason for living....We are guided and motivated by our hope for a future in which we can live fully.

Ada María Isasi-Díaz (1943–2012)

Like forgiveness, most people probably associate Jesus and Christianity with talk of a *kingdom* and the promise of *paradise*. They have good reason. On one hand, the Greek word for 'kingdom' – 'basileia' – occurs over 150 times in the New Testament. Most commonly, the New Testament speaks of 'the kingdom of God', although the Gospel of Matthew prefers the appellation 'the kingdom of heaven'. The New Testament sees Jesus as inaugurating this divine kingdom, whatever it may be. On the other hand, the Greek word for 'paradise' – 'parádeisos' – occurs on just three occasions in the New Testament. Nevertheless, 'paradise' carries as much potency as 'kingdom' in the Scriptures and for our imaginations. After all, the story of salvation that spans across the Old and New Testaments begins and ends in a paradisal garden. In the Genesis narrative, our primordial parent is placed in (and expelled from) the garden of Eden at the beginning of time (Genesis 2.8; 3.23). At the end of time, the Book of Revelation envisions that we are restored to paradise through Christ (Revelation 2.7; 22.1–5).

As we listen to this second last word shared between the thief and Christ, the 'kingdom' and the garden of 'paradise' move centre stage. 'Jesus, remember me when you come into your *kingdom*,' pleads the crucified thief. 'Truly I tell you,' Jesus replies, 'today you will be with me in *paradise*.' We are called to listen and understand what 'kingdom' and 'paradise' mean as they collide in this exchange on the cross. We are also called to wrestle with them as potential problems for how we face injustice in the world here and now.

In their distinct but overlapping ways, both 'kingdom' and 'paradise' intend to image the way God disrupts history. They signal God's making of something new. They dramatically interrupt, overturn and recreate the troubled present with the prospect of a new way of being. The 'kingdom' Jesus proclaims is 'not of this world' (John 18.36) – it is an entirely new, reimagined world of paradisal possibility. Spending a few moments with each word will explain what I mean here.

Jesus proclaims at the beginning of his ministry that the 'kingdom of God' has auspiciously drawn near (Mark 1.15). 'The time is fulfilled', he declares. The Greek word for 'time' in Mark's Gospel is 'kairos'. That word means something like an *opportune time or season*, namely one pregnant with new possibilities. In Christ, something *new* is happening in history that also signals the *end* of history, meaning the *fulfilment* of its promise for perfection. That something new is the 'kingdom of God'. Jesus understands his own purpose to be the good news of that kingdom (Luke 4.43). He accordingly sees the kingdom as being of paramount importance for believers. 'Strive first for the kingdom of God and his righteousness', Jesus exhorts the crowds who gather to hear him teach (Matthew 6.33). Jesus teaches his disciples to pray to the Father, 'your *kingdom* come' (Matthew 6.10).

The idea of the 'kingdom' dominates Jesus's parables. He sees it as something of utmost value, a 'treasure hidden in a field' and a 'pearl of great price' (Matthew 13.24, 44, 45, 47; cf. Mark 4.26, 30; Luke 19.11). The kingdom has the power to transform all things, like a mustard seed that grows into the 'greatest of shrubs' or a 'yeast' that leavens the whole. The 'kingdom of God' inverts all that we understand and accept as ordinary or inevitable in the world. Jesus teaches that 'blessed are the poor in spirit' and 'blessed are those who are persecuted' — for somehow 'theirs is the kingdom of heaven' (Matthew 5.3, 10). The kingdom of God has and will turn the world upside down. It restores right relationships between human beings, creation and God. It proclaims a divine grace and hope that breaks into the messiness of human history through Christ. This hope finds its consummation beyond that history. The kingdom of God *is an utterly new state of being in the presence of God*. It is a personal and social reality that is both 'now' insofar as it has broken into history through Christ, and 'not yet' insofar as it is yet to be fully realized. At the Last Supper, Jesus who inaugurates the kingdom nevertheless proclaims that 'I will never again drink of the fruit of the vine until that day when I drink it new in the kingdom of God' (Mark 14.25).

While the language of 'paradise' is comparatively rare in the New Testament, it similarly carries significant freight as the prevalent image of the 'kingdom' and overlaps closely with its meaning. Indeed, as the Italian philosopher Giorgio Agamben writes, it is 'not possible to separate the Garden from the Kingdom'. The New Testament understands 'paradise' in terms of its Jewish heritage. It evokes three notions at least: the garden of Eden; the temporary abode of the righteous; and a heavenly reward. In each case, however, the Christian tradition came to understand 'paradise' both as a *place* variously found in the past, present or future, and as a *blessed state of being that enjoys union with God*. In this sense, 'paradise' evokes similar ideas as the 'now but not yet' character of the 'kingdom of God'.

'Paradise' first recalls the mythic Eden or the 'garden of God' (Isaiah 51.3; Ezekiel 28.13) in which Adam and Eve were originally placed, and which they subsequently lost through disobedience (Genesis 3.22–4). While 'Eden' represented a place, Christians also understood it as a spiritual condition of radical intimacy with God. 'Adam was in paradise,' as the Orthodox theologian St Innocent of Alaska (1797–1879) put it, 'and paradise was in him.'

The impact of the expulsion from the garden of Eden became seen by early Christians as what Giorgio Agamben calls 'the determinative event of the human condition and the foundation of its economy of salvation'. The 'paradise in us' that our first parents lost, Christ regains as the 'new' Adam. Christ reconstitutes our human nature and unites it to the life of God (Romans 5.12–21; 1 Corinthians 15.22, 45). For the early Christians, sharing in Christ's life, death and resurrection re-opened paradise as a spiritual condition for the here and now, as well as a future promise of heavenly union. St Cyril of Jerusalem (313–386), for example, wrote of how baptism and the Eucharist united believers with Jesus and led them into the 'fragrant meadow of this present paradise'. In the Christian life, paradise breaks into the present. It begins to become a dynamic reality in which heaven and earth meet. Ephrem the Syrian (306–373) accordingly exhorted believers that 'while you are living, make yourself the key to paradise: that door desires you and gladly expects your arrival'.

Other first-century Jews imagined 'paradise' to be an abode for the souls of the righteous before the resurrection, sometimes called 'Abraham's bosom'. We hear a trace of this idea in the parable of the rich man and poor Lazarus (Luke 16.19–31). When the rich man and poor Lazarus die, the former experiences the torments of Hades. Looking up, the rich man sees 'Abraham far away with Lazarus by his side' (Luke 16.23). Abraham comforts Lazarus, consoling him for the way he suffered so much in life. Again, while 'paradise' or 'Abraham's bosom' represents a place, it involves spiritual consolation and intimacy. While this 'paradise' remains a post-mortem reality, it is one that we can intelligibly grasp. 'Paradise' demands of us a response as to how we ought to live in the here and now in light of eternity.

Other Jews and early Christians also thought of 'paradise' as a heavenly reward, or as the upper region of heaven, such as when St Paul describes how he was 'caught up to the third heaven…into Paradise' (2 Corinthians 12.1–4). 'Paradise' at times acted as a virtual synonym for God's heavenly rule at the end of the ages, namely the 'kingdom of God'. The entire story of God's saving acts in history would lead to this final state of righteousness. We hear a trace of this concept as Jesus proclaims that 'I tell you, many will come from east and west and will eat with Abraham and Isaac and Jacob in the kingdom of heaven' (Matthew 8.11). As with its other associations, 'paradise' takes on yet again the character both of a *present* spiritual reality and a *future* destination, a 'now' and 'not yet' held in tension.

In his second last word on the cross, Jesus promises this kind of paradise today to the criminal who pleads 'remember me when you come into your kingdom'. As with the first last word, the second last word is scandalous. That a failed messiah hanging on a cross could promise paradise today was laughable – and not least that he promises this to the scum of the earth pleading to be remembered in the kingdom of God.

We see the scandal of this second last word in different ways across the Gospels that describe those crucified alongside Jesus. The two people who are crucified either side of Jesus are recorded in the Gospels of Mark, Matthew, Luke and John. While John simply mentions them in passing, the Gospels of Mark and Matthew record how these two 'bandits' deride Jesus. Along with the chief priests, they play on the meaning of his name – Jesus, 'God saves' – to mock him. 'He saved others,' the taunt goes, 'he cannot save himself' (Mark 15.32; Matthew 27.42). The mockery is easy to understand. It's ridiculous that someone rendered powerless in the horror of crucifixion could promise entry into God's kingdom and paradise. It seems delusional. As Fleming Rutledge writes, the cross is 'a sign of weakness, ugliness, failure, incomprehension'. That the chosen one of Israel now gasps for life, broken on the cross, 'outside the camp' (Hebrews 13.13) where only the worst people are sent to brutal death, remains an uncomfortable, embarrassing and even farcical sight. It is scandalous that the crucified Jesus, in fulfilment of Isaiah's prophecy, is 'numbered among the transgressors' (Mark 15.28; cf. Isaiah 53.12).

In Luke's Gospel, however, the two thieves take on separate roles. They show another side to the scandal of this second last word. One thief reviles Jesus. He echoes the baying crowds in Mark and Matthew's Gospels. 'Are you not the Messiah?', he reproaches, 'save yourself and us!' (Luke 23.39). The other thief in Luke's Gospel, however, rebukes his fellow criminal. He sees the *innocence* of Jesus. Perhaps he has just heard Jesus pray to the Father to 'forgive them, for they do not know what they are doing'. He *sees* what others cannot

— a glimpse of *power in weakness*, the 'foolishness' of the cross that is 'the power of God' (1 Corinthians 1.24). The thief sees too his own *guilt*. He knows that he and his fellow bandit are 'condemned justly, for we are getting what we deserve for our deeds' (Luke 23.41). For this confession, the second thief is sometimes known as the 'penitent' or 'good' thief. He pleads to be remembered in God's kingdom — which means to be restored to right relations, with God and all, now and forever.

That Jesus promises paradise today to this kind of person remains shocking. We don't know the precise crimes the two criminals have committed. They are likely to have been extreme felonies. The Greek word variously translated as 'thief' or 'bandit' means something like 'plunderer', part of a roving and often murderous band whose members when caught would be given a death penalty under Roman law. Like Barabbas — who is also recorded as a 'bandit' in John's Gospel — the two crucified criminals may have been involved in armed and violent insurrection against the Romans. Either way — whether robbers or revolutionaries, or both — these men were bad news, scum and probably murderers. Some later theologians associated the thief with the murderer Cain, who in the Old Testament wanders 'east of Eden' after committing fratricide (Genesis 4.16). The thieves likewise stand firmly outside of paradise. That one of them then received the good news of the kingdom, restoring him to paradise, simply because he admits his guilt, was (and still is) offensive. The reward seems cheap. The promise of paradise seems too easy and crass considering the crimes of the thief. It seems like a tasteless affront and injustice to his victims.

What might we make, then, to the collision of a requested kingdom and a promised paradise in the exchange we overhear in this second last word? The terms do not translate easily or even well into modern frames of reference. We may struggle or even balk at them. We have all kind of learnt assumptions about the words 'paradise' and 'kingdom'. These learnt assumptions are not always favourable. They don't capture the range of ideas that the scriptural images intend to signal. On one hand, we might associate the idea of a 'kingdom' with pomp, power and privilege. It probably makes us think of distant kings and queens, of their endless schemes and squabbles. To speak of a 'kingdom' is to speak of the social inequalities they inscribe. It is an alien and anachronistic term for most of us. On the other hand, we might associate talk of 'paradise' with escapist fantasies of an imagined heavenly utopia, or with religious fundamentalism and its promise of heavenly reward for extreme beliefs. In both instances, neither 'kingdom' nor 'paradise' captures our popular imagination. They seem unpalatable, undesirable and outdated for a modern age.

Suspicion about the truth of religious claims about the 'kingdom' and 'paradise' feeds these popular learnt assumptions. These assumptions unwittingly echo the thought of another 'master of suspicion', the German political thinker and founding father of communism, Karl Marx. We ought to take these suspicions seriously. They give an insight into the ethical risks posed by religious talk about the 'kingdom of God' and 'paradise'. We might learn from these popular qualms, and the suspicious explanations of Marx. We might learn the *cost* of failing to attend to the radical *political* meaning of these theological concepts. These suspicions might *chasten* our religious understanding. They might also *save* us in practice from the seductive peril of over-spiritualizing the 'kingdom' and the 'garden' of paradise. They might allow us to *see* what the penitent thief saw on the cross – and be disrupted by that sight.

Marx infamously declared that 'religion is the opium of the people'. He saw religion as a problem for any political attempt to escape social inequality. Religion was a 'false consciousness' that made people avoid the need for revolutionary social change. Like Friedrich Nietzsche – another 'master of suspicion' – Marx's early life, however, was one marked by religion. His paternal and maternal grandfathers were both rabbis. Marx's family converted from Judaism to Christianity before he was born. The conversion was socially expedient, helping the family avoid antisemitic laws and persecution. Unsurprisingly, perhaps, Marx rejected Christianity early in his life and became an avowed atheist. Like Nietzsche, it was in Marx's university days that he sought to understand the origin and problem of religion. Two thinkers influenced Marx, and we can turn to each to unpack his suspicious explanation of religious language. Suspicion was part of his political awakening to social ills and inequalities. Like Nietzsche, what Marx sought was an alternative form of salvation to what he saw as Christianity's illusory promise of an otherworldly justice. In Marx's case, true salvation was political revolution leading to economic freedom. Marx's philosophical project was not merely to interpret the world rightly – 'the point is to change it', he wrote, an epigraph that would eventually adorn his gravestone.

The first major influence on Marx was Georg Wilhelm Friedrich Hegel (1770–1831), a German philosopher and one of the founding figures of modern philosophy. Hegel's philosophy was complex, but two basic ideas shaped Marx's imagination, even if he significantly adapted Hegel's thought. The first idea was that of the character of history. For Hegel, history tended towards human freedom. The second idea was that of 'dialectic'. For Hegel, 'dialectic' describes the process of this historical arc that bends towards freedom. We might think of 'dialectic' as being like a critical dialogue between opposing ideas that produces a new understanding. While Hegel didn't quite put it this way, people sometimes label the 'dialectical method' in terms of thesis, anti-thesis and synthesis. We take some original idea or *thesis*. We then take an alternative *anti-thesis* opposed to that original idea. Then, we see a *synthesis* emerge that resolves the tension between the thesis and its anti-thesis at a higher level of truth. Hegel thought that every age showed the inexorable historical movement towards freedom through this kind of dialectical process. Ideas competed with one another, leading to truth that sets people free. In fact, history was simply the vessel for the spiritual unfolding of inevitable freedom.

For Marx, Hegel was right, but had things turned upside down. Hegel was broadly right about how to understand historical change. Yet, Hegel mistakenly abstracted and spiritualized the process of change. For Marx, history tended not just towards individual human freedom, but towards freedom in community. Human beings could not be understood abstractly. Rather, they are made up by their social relations. Human freedom implied, then, addressing the concrete social conditions for humans flourishing together. Furthermore, for Marx, the dialectical process of human progress was not a mental one about ideas that inevitably led to change as a matter of divine providence. Rather, the dialectical process was one grounded in the material realities of communities and involved intentional political conflict. The motor of history was not ideas and philosophers as such. It was the economic relations between people and the perspective of the exploited worker. The growing social and economic inequalities of his age led to Marx arguing that 'the history of all hitherto existing societies is the history of class struggles'. For Marx, a new stage of political history would emerge from the dialectical confrontation in his age between capitalism and socialism – namely, the communism he envisaged and the call to revolution he embraced. 'The proletarians [workers] have nothing to lose but their chains,' the Communist Manifesto of 1848 rallied, 'they have a world to win!' As Marx saw it, communism provided a harmonious and just vision of social life in which each person contributes and receives according to her ability and needs.

The second major influence on Marx was Ludwig Feuerbach (1804–1872), the same radical German philosopher who impacted Nietzsche too. Marx took from him the idea that 'man makes religion, religion does not make man'. Feuerbach argued that we can understand 'religion' as a spiritual projection of material realities and desires. From Feuerbach, Marx could critique religion from within the understanding of historical change he adapted from Hegel. Marx added to Feuerbach's insight, however, a social and political aspect. This aspect made religion into a political *problem* for those who sought radical change. As we've seen, for Marx, we can only understand 'human nature' in its social context. 'Man,' he wrote, 'is the world of man, state, society.' In other words, 'human nature' is 'the ensemble of social relations' and not some abstract essence. Human *society* – and not an abstracted human nature – produces religion as an expression of itself. Religion describes social relations but also inscribes inequalities by providing a 'spiritual aroma' to the world. As Marx wanted to critique the inequalities of western societies, then, he saw that all criticism had to begin with the criticism of religion. He would avow that 'the criticism of religion is, therefore, in embryo, the criticism of that vale of tears of which religion is the halo'.

Marx's attitude to, and critique of, religion was more nuanced than is often allowed. On the one hand, religion was 'the sigh of the oppressed creature, the heart of a heartless world, and the soul of soulless conditions'. Religion named the lived experience of social inequality and questioned what must be done. It did not hide the reality of suffering. It was a protest. Yet, religion also *numbed* people to suffering. Religion gave the wrong answer to the right question. Religion inhibited people from trying to *change* society by promising some imagined, future, otherworldly resolution to social ills. As such, religion was the 'opium of the people'. Marx taught us to be suspicious about religious language of the kingdom and paradise. Religion deterred determined human action for actual liberation in the here and now. 'The more of himself man gives to God,' Marx wrote, 'the less he has left in himself.' As such, religion produced a false consciousness based upon an illusory promise. 'The abolition of religion as the illusory happiness of the people,' Marx wrote, 'is the demand for their *real* happiness.' Indeed, religion was a conservative social force that could so easily legitimate social and economic exploitation as something that was part of a supposedly divine order. 'The parson,' Marx averred, 'has ever gone hand in hand with the landlord.' To face up to reality and strive for radical change, Marx thought, was true salvation. In doing so, people would be saved from social oppression undergirded by religious illusion. They would be saved for a new way of being under communism as the true 'end of history'.

Whatever we may think of his broader political philosophy, Marx's suspicious explanation of religion keeps us *honest*. Marx makes us face up to what we mean when we speak of the 'kingdom of God' and 'paradise'. He asks uncomfortable questions about whether we take them seriously as realities that might exist not just in the future but *today*. The 'kingdom' and the 'garden' voice a vision with radical implications that we all too rarely hear or see in Christian communities. Marx saw that. Christianity through the ages is replete with uneasy examples of the close alliance of religion with established power. Those who dare to draw out the radical implications of the 'kingdom' and 'garden' as political realities that might overturn established patterns of power have typically been dismissed and persecuted as heretics and extremists.

The same uneasy alliance between religion and power remains true in our own age too. We can still see unfolding before our eyes what Agamben calls the 'dominant strategy... to neutralize [the] political implications' of the 'kingdom' and 'paradise'. Christianity has undoubtedly legitimated violence, oppression and inequality in the past and present. All too often it defers justice to some imagined future, heavenly realm. Christians fall prey to the seductive temptation to give the soothing balm of a future promise, rather than joining in outrage at injustice and forging tools for change *today*. As Marx saw, Christianity and its Scriptures describe the cries of injustice experienced by people and express a longing for a different world. Christianity then fails to *change* the world. Insofar as this remains true, Christianity is part of the social problems of any age.

Little wonder, then, that in the popular imagination, neither 'the kingdom of God' nor the promise of 'paradise' hold much power or interest these days. Very few churches talk about either the kingdom or the garden in any meaningful way that impacts upon the immediate realities of people. Christians have lost the radical vision of what the thief in this second last word *saw* in Christ as he pleaded to be remembered in God's kingdom. Too few Christians wrestle with making the promise of paradise into a reality for *today*.

Marx makes us face squarely, then, the failure of Christianity to attend fully to the second last word on the cross. He challenges how we should live in the face of actual suffering and injustice. Marx's voice remains a *prophetic* one in that he sees what others cannot or will not. He speaks truth to power. We ought to listen to him as a religious imperative. As John Raines puts it, Marx is 'like the Hebrew prophets' of the Old Testament insofar as he 'was driven by a passion for truth and for justice'. Raines continues that 'like the Hebrew prophets of old, Marx knew that to speak of social justice we must become socially self-critical, and that means becoming critical of the ruling powers – whether they be kings or priests or investment bankers'. Indeed, for Marx, 'like the prophets before him, the most revealing perspective is…the view of the "widow and orphan" – the point of view of the exploited and marginalized'. Marx's suspicious explanation of religion demands *honesty* about religion's capacity to be complicit with power, inequality and suffering. His suspicious explanation recalls the prophetic insight that religion protests oppression. Protest can pierce the veil of power to reveal truth and a different way of being. If salvation means anything, it must include the redemption of actual bodies and societies. Yet, Marx reminds us that all too often prophets and their messages are *killed* by religion too. Little wonder that in practice Christians shy away from the challenge.

Yet, while Marx gives the right *diagnosis*, he follows with a *prognosis* that is contestable and perhaps even reductive. In other words, he rightly calls Christians to account for the dangers inherent in their language. He shows the way in which religious talk of a 'kingdom' and 'paradise' can render people inert and engender a fatalistic acceptance of the way things are in this life. Marx fails, however, to see the intrinsic and radical potential of that language nevertheless. Talk of a 'kingdom' and 'paradise' *can* change the world in the revolutionary way he saw as a necessary feature of salvation. This talk can change the world if we take it *seriously*. This second last word calls us to attend to the radical request and promise so that we reorient our view of the world and the character of our faith. Christianity is not necessarily a just moribund phenomenon, a 'false consciousness' that will die away once people address the real causes of social and economic injustice. Christianity has the explosive potential to be the conduit for social transformation.

We can wrestle with this possibility by returning to the second last word on the cross. Marx's prognosis for religion, and our negative learnt assumptions, are not what Jesus or the New Testament writers mean when they talk of the 'kingdom of God' or of 'paradise'. We need to disambiguate both words from their possible negative connotations and the seductive temptations that Marx decried. We need to recapture something of the radically disruptive spirit of this second last word on the cross and its colliding images of a 'kingdom' and a 'paradise'. It is a moral imperative to do so. It will not just *describe* the world – it will *change* it.

The Hispanic practical theologian Elizabeth Conde-Frazier offers us some help with understanding what the New Testament means when it uses the word 'kingdom'. She writes that 'the kingdom of God' is 'neither a territorial realm in the present nor a promised realm that exists only in the future'. The 'kingdom of God' bears no similarity with earthly kingdoms found across history. It 'does not belong to this world', as Jesus puts it (John 18.36). Rather, Conde-Frazier explains how the 'kingdom of God' is 'a dynamic in which the power of God is enacted'. This divine dynamic has a present inner and a future outer aspect. We keep both aspects in view as we hear the crucified thief ask for the 'kingdom of God' and as Jesus promises that 'today you will be with me in paradise'.

In the present inner aspect, the 'kingdom of God' is 'among you' or 'within you' (Luke 17.21). It refers to the mutual indwelling of believers and Christ. As people abide in

Jesus, he abides in them. The kingdom of God is a rule of the heart. It is more than a pretty metaphor. This inner dynamic of mutual indwelling transforms the believer such that she is 'conformed to the image' of Jesus (Romans 8.29) and transformed by love (2 Corinthians 3.18). The 'parables of the kingdom' revolve around the utter worth and inestimable value of a life centred in Christ who is the fullness of life (Matthew 13.24–33). The crucified thief pleads that this life of being 'in Christ' as a 'new creation' (2 Corinthians 5.17) might be true for him as he takes his final pained breaths.

In the future outer aspect, the 'kingdom of God' also describes the final flowering of all things in that love and because of that indwelling. It is a future social event to be anticipated, but one that is 'close at hand' (Mark 1.5; Matthew 3.2, 4.17, 10.7; Luke 10. 9, 11, 21.28, 31). It is a divine pledge to honour and recreate all things. It is the lived social reality of a world transformed by grace. It is the promise of what has broken in through Christ and what God will bring to fulfilment. In the end – in the fullness of time – the kingdom of God is paradise regained. As we walk with the scars and marks of mortality, it is God's promise that we will 'eat from the tree of life that is in the paradise of God' (Revelation 2.7). So too, then, does the thief ask to be *remembered* – re-made – in this promise as he turns to Jesus while darkness falls on the whole land. If all of humanity – and especially the worst excesses we are capable of – are not taken into the kingdom, then there will always be something still to save. It is shocking that Jesus promises paradise to the thief. But that is the promise of the kingdom to redeem all things. Indeed, it is the promise of the incarnation. As Gregory of Nazianzus

(c. 329–390) put it, what Jesus 'has not assumed [meaning, what he has taken on in his humanity], he has not healed'.

In both its present inner and future outer aspects, the 'kingdom of God' represents a *gift*, but also a *risk* should we take it seriously.

The 'kingdom of God' is not a reward for good behaviour as such. It is the offering of a new way, with God as its architect, donor and guarantor. It describes the radical priority of God's gracious action to redeem, restore and elevate humanity and all of creation fallen into disorder. It is a gift – a vision – that involves challenging the status quo. It is a gift and vision for every nook and corner of creation. It touches even the body of the penitent thief.

The 'kingdom of God' and its 'paradise' are highly subversive terms, both in their own historical context and for us. They mean taking risks and embracing scandal for the sake of the vision of a new way. For Jesus and his followers to speak of the 'kingdom of God' and 'paradise' – and to refer to Jesus as 'Lord' – was revolutionary. They lived in a violent and oppressive imperial age of Roman conquest and power in which allegiance and obedience was due to Caesar as Lord. As the biblical scholar William Carter puts it, 'the Gospel depicts God's salvation, the triumph of God's empire over all things, including Rome, with the language and symbols of imperial rule'. To speak of the 'kingdom of God' shakes the violence of the present with the presence of God and the promise of paradise. It was to unveil as a sham the imperial claim that the Roman Empire produced peace, the so-called *pax Romana*. What that earthly kingdom really represented was tyranny, cruelty and inequality. Whatever the two bandits have done that led to their crucifixion, they have been caught up in this terror. The kingdom and the garden expose the perversity of the status quo and image an alternative reality.

The 'kingdom of God' remains the reason why Jesus was crucified by the occupying Roman imperial forces. It subverted the privilege, power, prestige and peace of a human economy predicated upon violence, oppression and inequality. It threatened the status quo. It retains that subversive quality in our age too, should we accept it as a new reality and a new thing created in Christ. In this second last word, the penitent thief, subjected to the violent and dehumanizing death of the Roman Empire, asks for a new thing. Jesus promises it – not simply in some imagined future but even as a paradise today. That promise is the challenge this second last word presents to those who see in Christ what the second thief saw.

The radical potential of the 'kingdom of God' and 'paradise' heard in this second last word is also seen in the *bodies* who speak from one cross to another. We should not forget that both Jesus and the thief as Jews lived under the brutal colonial rule of the Roman Empire. Colonial power has a psychological as well as a material dimension. In their daily lives, Jesus and the thief were oppressed by the sword and by the mind. Their entire existence was one of imperial subjugation. They both experienced the brutal physical and psychological realities of that oppression in their crucifixion at the hands of the occupying Roman forces. Indeed, crucifixion was typically reserved for non-Roman people. The crucifixion of colonial subjects enacted how they were less than human, objects of control and scorn. The physical and mental torture of crucifixion displayed their inhumanity in extreme and visceral fashion.

We too live, of course, in the shadows of empire in our own age, albeit the legacy of modern European rather than ancient Roman imperialism. The huge raising of consciousness around race and empire in recent years unveil the vicious ways that power distorts societies. The racist legacy of western imperialism continues to oppress the bodies and minds of minority ethnic/global majority heritage communities. The Kenyan writer Ngũgĩ wa Thiong'o (b. 1938) writes that 'the bullet was the means of the physical subjugation [of western colonialism]' but 'language was the means of spiritual subjugation'. It was not enough to control the bodies of colonized subjects. Colonial power had to colonize the mind too. Colonial power had to assimilate and dominate everything. It had to subjugate the whole person, to cast them as inferior, as scum, as less than human. We continue to live in a society shaped by the heresy of racism that underpinned European colonial expansion.

The thief and Jesus *dare* to imagine a different and new way of being that cuts against the oppressive imperial grain that had broken their bodies and minds. What the thief and Jesus in this second last word dare to imagine is the liberation of bodies and minds in a brave new world. This liberation explodes the status quo. It imagines a future that can begin even now, today, should we just ask for it and be inspired by the promise of it. What the thief and Jesus dare to speak is what we are called to dare to speak too in our own postcolonial age.

The final word of this chapter should belong, then, to the Hispanic *mujerista* theologian, Ada María Isasi-Díaz. She was born in Cuba, but later moved to the United States as a political refugee. Isasi-Díaz was aware of how sexism, ethnic prejudice and economic oppression subjugate women and people of global majority heritage, both in society and churches. For Isasi-Díaz, Christianity nevertheless offered not only a language of protest against real suffering, but also the means to *change* the world. Christians had to wrestle with the moral urgency of what Christ's life, death and resurrection meant for the world here and now. She rejected the word 'kingdom' because of the negative connotations of the word. 'The concept of [the] kingdom [of God] in our world today,' she wrote, 'is both hierarchical and elitist – which is why I do not use the word reign.' Instead, Isasi-Díaz talked about the 'kin-dom of God'. 'The word *kin-dom* makes it clear,' she explained, 'that when the fullness of God becomes a day-to-day reality in the world at large, we will all be sisters and brothers – kin to each other.'

Isasi-Díaz's vision of the 'kin-dom of God' is one of liberation. It assumes the disruptive activity of God breaking into history and the messiness of actual human communities. The 'kin-dom' offers a vision that does not defer action – it directs where we are going. 'We are guided and motivated,' she wrote, 'by our hope for a future in which we can live fully.' The vision of the 'kin-dom' is not a sedative against action. It does not defer the resolution of injustice to some heavenly future. The vision allows us to see what the second thief saw in Jesus on the cross. It is a vision for change that inspires movement, action, revolution, a complete turning around of the status quo. The 'kin-dom' sets a question mark against all that is. It expresses the hope of all that the world might be. It frees bodies and minds for the fullness of life together. It is the promise of God for something new. It is the demand on us made by the world. It is a radical risk — and hope.

The challenge of this second last word — and of Isasi-Díaz — is simple but profound and life-changing. Will we strive first for the 'kin-dom of God,' above all else, taking all the risks it involves? Dare we ask for what the thief does as our preferred future? Dare we trust in the promise of paradise he hears from Jesus as our unfolding reality *now*? Dare we have faith that what we begin today, God will honour at the end of time? Do we have the courage to be where Christ is and where the thief is going?

3

'BEHOLD'

Meanwhile, standing near the cross of Jesus were his mother, and his mother's sister, Mary the wife of Clopas and Mary Magdalene. When Jesus saw his mother and the disciple whom he loved standing beside her, he said to his mother, 'Woman, here is your son.' Then he said to the disciple, 'Here is your mother.' And from that hour the disciple took her into his own home.

John 19.25–7

Violent, irrational, intolerant, allied to racism and tribalism and bigotry, invested in ignorance and hostile to free inquiry, contemptuous of women and coercive toward children: organized religion ought to have a great deal on its conscience.

Christopher Hitchens (1949–2011)

The cross represents the power that denigrates human bodies, destroys life and preys on the most vulnerable in society. As the cross is defeated, so too is that power.

Kelly Brown Douglas

The third last word revolves around the power of *sight*. The first two last words spoken on the cross imagine a new way of being. The first last word imagines a way of being flowing from forgiveness. The second last word imagines a way of being that single-mindedly pursues the alternative preferred future of the kingdom of God and paradise. Now, the third last word calls us to *see* this new way of being breaking in right before our eyes.

What we *see* as Jesus commends his mother and his beloved disciple to each other is the making of new relations configured by *kinship*. 'Here is your son,' Jesus says to his mother. 'Here is your mother,' Jesus says to his beloved disciple, the precise identity of whom is disputed. We might better translate the original Greek – as many older translations do – as '*behold* your mother' and '*behold* your son'. *Behold* – Jesus commands a new sight. He invites his mother and beloved disciple to *see* in one another a bond 'born, not of blood' but 'of God' (John 1.13). Jesus opens eyes to the sight of true kinship. As we may recall, kinship is how Ada María Isasi-Díaz translates the idea of the 'kingdom of God' sounded in the second last word. The kingdom – the *kin-dom* – sought by the crucified criminal in the second last word now erupts into reality in this third last word. Through Jesus, Mary and the beloved disciple are made one – they become a new family.

It comes as little surprise, then, that Christianity abounds with the language of *family, community* and *belonging* as part of a new identity in Christ. After all, this is the *kinship* that Jesus calls us to *see* in this third last word. St Paul writes that Jesus is the 'firstborn within a large family' (Romans 8.29). St Paul elsewhere describes the early followers of Jesus as 'God's

family' and as the 'family of faith' (Galatians 1.2, 6.10).
St Peter commends his fellow believers to 'honour everyone'
and 'love the family of believers' (1 Peter 2.17). There are
numerous references across the New Testament to the early
churches being the 'people of God', a term with Jewish roots
describing the chosen or favoured community of God (e.g.,
2 Corinthians 6.16; Hebrews 4.9, 11.25; Revelation 21.3).

The images of family, community and belonging are not
just pretty metaphors. Through baptism, people 'belong
to Jesus Christ' (Romans 1.6). As people 'belong' to Jesus,
they 'belong' to Christ's 'body', an image St Paul uses to
describe the Church as the social extension of Jesus (e.g.,
1 Corinthians 12.12–27; Ephesians 3.6, 5.23; Colossians
1.18, 24). Baptism incorporates believers into Christ as their
identity and reality. Baptism translates them into the Church
as a new family founded in and by Christ. In this new family,
diversity remains essential for the flourishing of the whole
body. 'So we, who are many,' St Paul writes, 'are one body
in Christ, and individually we are members one of another'
(Romans 12.5). Christians call one another 'brother' and
'sister', titles not given by biology but by the blood of Christ.
Being one in Christ unites all differences. 'There is no longer
Jew or Greek,' writes St Paul, 'there is no longer slave or
free, there is no longer male and female; for all of you are one
in Christ Jesus's (Galatians 3.28). Baptism adopts believers
through Christ into the life of God in all its fullness. Christ
'has given us everything needed for life and godliness',
St Peter writes, that we 'may become participants of the
divine nature' (2 Peter 1.3). Through Christ, we are kin, not
only with one another, but with God. We are called to see

and live this kinship through the Church as the social Body of Christ. This sight brings the vision of the kin-dom of God into view as our reality. It is why the American theologian Stanley Hauerwas can proclaim confidently that 'the church does not *have* a social ethic; the church *is* a social ethic'.

Not everyone *sees* anything like this positive vision of kinship, of course, when they are faced with actual Christian communities. In fact, they may see the opposite. They may see religions and religious communities as a source of social disease rather than as the cure for such social ills. Engaging with these negative perceptions and experiences keeps Christian communities *honest*. After all, they are real perceptions and experiences, even if they are hard to hear or perhaps do not represent the whole story.

The most potent form of these criticisms can be found in the contemporary New Atheists. Emerging at the turn of the twenty-first century, the New Atheists have gained much media, popular and scholarly attention in recent decades. They have gained such traction in part because they capture and articulate popular suspicions about religious belief fuelled by the patent moral failures of religions.

The most famous proponents of New Atheism are a group of scientists, philosophers and journalists styled as the 'four horsemen of the apocalypse'. These 'four horsemen' are Richard Dawkins, Daniel Dennett, Sam Harris and the late Christopher Hitchens. Their works have often proved international bestsellers. Critics of New Atheism often dismiss it as 'a repackaging of age-old philosophical arguments combined with an intolerant, dogmatic and aggressively anti-religious rhetoric', as one commentator summarizes it.

Yet, New Atheism captures at least one vital thing regarding religious claims about belief and belonging to which we must attend. There is, has been and can be a significant *moral gap* between how Christianity understands itself, and how far from that ideal its communal reality can be.

If we are to see the kinship that this third last word commands as authentic, we must wrestle with the New Atheist critique of religion and take it seriously. We must grapple with the hard facts about how Christian communities operate. New Atheism makes us squarely face the painful dissonance between a Christian ideal of kinship and the reality that 'the life of the church is a series of always failing experiments', as the contemporary theologian Mike Higton evocatively puts it.

What, then, is 'New Atheism' and what does it argue? 'New Atheism' is more a loose sensibility than a precisely defined movement. Even the name remains a little misleading. It's hard to pinpoint what exactly is new about the New Atheists. Given the long, variegated and complex history of atheism, New Atheists do not give any critique of religion that is necessarily new as such. There is no consensus about what New Atheism precisely is. We can point, however, to recurring commitments and themes. The New Atheists stress how dispassionate reason and science provide the best means of understanding reality as it is. They argue that religions are not only irrational but pathological and dangerous. They call for an end to religious belief as either credible or desirable.

It's more accurate, then, to call the New Atheists *anti-theists* rather than atheists. The New Atheists do not simply deny that God exists. Rather, they argue that religious belief is both intellectually indefensible and causes all kinds of social evils. As evidence, they point to things like the medieval Crusades, the history of interminable wars of religion, the suicidal fanaticism of religious extremists, religious 'texts of terror' that justify oppression, the incredulity of certain religious claims, and the moral hypocrisy of leading religious figures. The New Atheists oppose, then, the ongoing existence of religious belief and practice essentially on *moral* grounds. For the New Atheists, religion inhibits true human flourishing. The New Atheists seek the end of religion as a viable option in a modern, pluralistic world.

Like Nietzsche and Marx, the New Atheists aim to save us from religion. If there is anything new about 'New Atheism', it is the *political* turn in this redemptive quest. New Atheists advocate for the separation of church and state, equal protection under law for atheists, and free criticism of religious beliefs and practices. The New Atheists seek to save people for a world marked by human freedom, limited only by how far we 'dare to know' or 'have courage to use our own understanding', as the German Enlightenment philosopher Immanuel Kant (1724–1804) put it.

The range and number of New Atheists and their publications makes a comprehensive survey and analysis impossible here. We can listen to a sample, however, to better grasp what their common themes sound like. Spending a few moments with each of the 'four horsemen of the apocalypse' will demonstrate how an intellectual critique of religious claims quickly take on a political character about the negative moral impact of religions on society – and a clarion call to reject religion all together.

As a first example, Daniel Dennett offered a trenchant philosophical critique of religion in *Darwin's Dangerous Idea*, first published in 1995. In *Darwin's Dangerous Idea*, Dennett argues that Darwin's theory of evolution acts as a 'universal acid'. This universal acid 'eats through just about every traditional concept and leaves in its wake a revolutionized worldview, with most of the old landmarks still recognizable, but transformed in fundamental ways'. What Dennett means is something like the following. If we want to understand how there is a diversity of species, Darwin's theory of evolution provides a sufficient explanatory framework. Darwin's theory of evolution argues that all species arise and develop through the natural selection of inherited characteristics that increase an individual's ability to compete for limited resources, survive a hostile world and reproduce. As Dennett develops Darwin's thought, we can see how such evolution occurs as a 'mindless, algorithmic process' – which means through purposeless, mechanical processes. We do not need to posit a creator God whose mind designs the universe to render creation as intelligible.

For Dennett, science, rather than religion, provides us with a universally accessible and rationally demonstrable way to understand the world. Science opens our eyes to reality and its complexity. 'There is no future in a sacred myth,' Dennett concludes. There is no need or room for God, other than as a comforting but ultimately infantile story. Comforting and infantile – but also *dangerous* in the way that religion breeds dogmatic certainty. 'I for one am not in awe of your faith,' Dennett elsewhere objects, 'I am appalled by your arrogance, by your unreasonable certainty that you have all the answers.'

In *The God Delusion*, first published in 2006, Richard Dawkins similarly challenges religion, moving from an intellectual to a moral critique of religion. Dawkins argues that the idea of a creator God who designs all things generates an unanswerable problem of infinite regression. 'The designer hypothesis,' Dawkins writes, 'immediately raises the larger problem of who designed the designer.' In other words, if God made the world, then who made God? Now, Christian theologians have long argued that God is an 'uncaused cause' or 'unmoved mover,' meaning that God has no creator and there is nothing prior to God. Yet, this theological claim cannot be in any sense scientifically *proven*. For Dawkins, Darwin's idea of natural selection offers an alternative, elegantly simple, verifiable and self-sufficient explanation of why there is a diversity of species.

From here Dawkins pivots, however, to a more explicitly anti-theistic stance. Dawkins offers a naturalistic account for the existence of religion. He proposes a 'theory of religion as an accidental by-product – a misfiring of something useful'. For Dawkins, things like morality are caused not by religion as such but by altruistic genes, selected through the process of evolution, that give people natural empathy and promote the survival of the human species. For Dawkins, religions historically emerged as a social product that could legitimate these moral codes by appealing to God as their source. Now we know, however, these moral codes appeared as a product of evolution, not God. Evolution renders religion redundant as an explanatory framework. Redundant – but also *dangerous*. Indeed, as they operate in society, religions represent a 'divisive force…a label for in-group/out-group enmity and vendetta'. For Dawkins, religions subvert science, encourage violence and legitimate repressive and oppressive bigotry around human sexuality and beyond. Tellingly, *The God Delusion* concludes with a list of resources for those 'needing support in *escaping* religion'.

The writings of Sam Harris (a philosopher and neuroscientist) and Christopher Hitchens (a journalist and literary critic) offer further intellectual and moral critiques of religious belief and communities that we can sample.

'In a world riven by ignorance,' Sam Harris writes, 'only the atheist refuses to deny the obvious: religious faith promotes human violence to an astonishing degree.' Harris unpacks this moral critique of faith-based religion in *The End of Faith*, published in 2004. He wrote the book in the wake of the September 11 attacks in 2001 by Islamist terrorists. Harris criticizes the allegedly violent character of Islam, but then turns his gaze to other faith-based religions like Christianity. As he surveys the history of faith-based religions, Harris sees just how mortally dangerous religious beliefs are. For Harris, this is the rule rather than the exception for faith-based religions. Whether moderate or extreme, any religious belief struggles to compromise when it comes to conflict or disagreement. For Harris, this is because faith is fundamentally irrational, dogmatic and incapable of openness. As such, faith fuels division, conflict, oppression and violence. The title of his book, then, represents a moral imperative – we must stop accepting faith as reasonable or as desirable, and instead seek its end. 'The only angels we need invoke,' Harris writes, 'are those of our better nature: reason, honesty, and love.' Likewise, 'the only demons we must fear are those that lurk inside every human mind: ignorance, hatred, greed, and *faith*, which is surely the devil's masterpiece.'

Finally, Christopher Hitchens offers a similar damning portrayal of religion in *God is not Great*, published in 2007. In the US version, it carried the subtitle 'how religion poisons everything'. In this work, Hitchens seeks to draw out this venom and cure the reader of religion. Hitchens styles his work as the completion of the Enlightenment critique of religious belief and religion. The 'exceptional claims' of religion, Hitchens writes, 'demand exceptional evidence' – which is profoundly lacking, he thinks. As such, 'what can be asserted without evidence', he continues, 'can also be dismissed without evidence'.

It is not enough, however, Hitchens thinks, to point out the incredulity of religious belief. Those religious beliefs legitimate *violence*. Hitchens holds up a scathing mirror to religions: 'Violent, irrational, intolerant, allied to racism and tribalism and bigotry, invested in ignorance and hostile to free inquiry, contemptuous of women and coercive toward children: organized religion ought to have a great deal on its conscience.' In short, religion *kills* – and now must be *killed* by critical scrutiny. 'Religion,' Hitchens concludes, 'has run out of justifications' and a 'new enlightenment' can save us from it for good.

One way or another, we will have strong responses to the New Atheist critique of religious rationality and the way it presents communities of faith. We may be quick to agree with New Atheism. We may see no future for irrational and morally flawed religious communities. Or we may rush to object. We may seek to drown New Atheism with a sea of words that refute its arguments. Or we may struggle to know what to think or how to respond.

One thing, however, that no one can or should deny are historical facts – religious communities have and do exclude, oppress and murder. This is not to say, of course, that religious communities are never on the side of the angels, do good or change human society for the better. We would, however, be trapped in self-deception and lack credibility if we brush aside history. The troubled and troubling history of religious communities that New Atheism exposes so brutally should cause us to doubt the moral credibility of communities of faith. The suspicious explanation of religion given by New Atheism – and its strident rejection of religion – deserve and demand a response that does more than reject criticism or look for false equivalences to excuse moral failure in religious communities. 'It is interesting to find,' Hitchens once caustically observed, 'that people of faith now seek defensively to say that they are no worse than Nazis or Stalinists.' If people of faith are to respond to the New Atheist moral objection against religious belief, they must wrestle with the religious history of and capacity for destructive violence in a more convincing way.

Like other suspicious explanations of religion that we have engaged so far, the *diagnosis* of New Atheism is right. That does not render as inevitable, however, their terminal *prognosis* for religious communities. Returning to what we *see* in this third last word reveals how violence gives birth to the cross. It also unveils how the cross gives birth to a non-violent kinship.

The sight of this kinship in this third last word might appear incongruous at first. After all, the violent brutality of the cross is the site of this sight. Yet what we see even in the terror

of crucifixion has the power to *disrupt* everything with a new
communal reality made by Jesus. That new communal reality
interrupts the world. It puts a question mark over the way
the world dominates, destroys and deals death to communal
bonds of kinship. What New Atheism unflinchingly demands
we see is how that new communal reality must also interrupt
religious communities too. It stands as a question mark over
the ways in which actual Christian communities also fail to
behold the radical sight that Jesus commands.

At first view, what we *see* on the cross, of course, is the
horrific power of state violence fuelled by religious division.
An unholy alliance of power and religion have conspired to
kill Jesus in a brutal way. The cross represents the horrendous
evil experienced not only by Jesus but by those who love
him as a collective trauma. The horrific power of crucifixion
wrenches limbs and crushes souls. It stakes out oppressive
human claims to power through staking bodies to a cross.
As Jesus speaks this third last word, we see Christ's body
shattered. We see his community scattered. Only a few
followers remain to see and experience the trauma unfold
before their eyes. In John's Gospel, the few who remain
stand not at a distance (as Mark 15.40–1 describes it) but
'near the cross of Jesus'. The crucifixion is their immediate
and brutal reality – it unfolds within their close sight. The
cross crucifies them as much as Jesus.

In John's Gospel, only three women and one man stay
as faithful witnesses to the terror of Jesus's death. The
crucifixion is an unimaginable sight and psychological
trauma for them, just as much as it is a brutal physical
torture for Jesus. These faithful four mirror the four Roman

soldiers who crucify Jesus and divide his clothing just before we hear this third last word. They stand as *victims* of the forces of death and destruction that tear apart bonds of family and friendship. One of these faithful four is Jesus's mother, Mary, the one whom Simeon prophesied would one day feel a sword 'pierce your own soul too' on account of her son (Luke 2.35). The hour of the cross is that day for Mary. Another who remains close to the cross is the one called 'the beloved disciple' in John's Gospel. The adjective 'beloved' indicates what matters most. Like Mary, this is someone whose heart is pierced by a sword of grief too. The trauma of the cross cascades through Jesus's circles of care and support. It is hard to believe we could see any good news as the crisis of the cross unfolds. In the cross, we see how the violence of social and religious power kills human bonds of affection and care.

What Jesus speaks, however, in this third last word to his mother and beloved disciple invites another vision. This vision disrupts what they and we see at first, much as the first two last words disrupt how we conceive of God, others and ourselves. In this new sight, the four faithful watchers become a critical foil. They stand *against* the violence of the four Roman soldiers. As Jesus speaks, we can see the violence of the cross does not have the last word at all. It does not present the only possible vision.

Behold, Jesus says. It is a command. *Open your eyes in this hour of the cross.* This command arrests the sight of Mary and the beloved disciple within the faithful four at the foot of the cross. It directs their eyes to a *new sight*. He calls them to see *kinship* in this terrible moment of trauma. This sight disrupts the visceral view of human brokenness which at first seizes their gaze – and ours too.

It is simultaneously easy to underestimate and to over-interpret the command to *behold* given in this third last word.

On the one hand, what we see might seem little more than 'an adoption arrangement', as Pope Benedict XVI puts it. In this third last word, Jesus provides for his vulnerable and traumatized mother. Jesus ensures that Mary has a home and someone to take his role as her son. This is precisely how the early Church often interpreted this third last word. Both Cyril of Alexandria (376–444) and St John Chrysostom (347–407) saw this third last word as Jesus simply fulfilling the commandment to honour your parents. This 'adoption' of Mary responds to her need for consolation and care. It is immediately recognizable as a very human response to very human needs. We might imagine ourselves giving the response that the beloved disciple does. For example, the fifteenth-century mystic Margery Kempe in a vision consoles Mary that the sufferings of Jesus are over. Like the beloved disciple, Margery takes Mary home and gives 'a good caudle of broth to comfort her'.

The 'adoption arrangement' of this third last word also honours the beloved disciple. Jesus also provides for the practical needs of his beloved disciple. Jesus entrusts his mother to the disciple's care, but also commends the disciple to Mary's care, thereby 'making him His brother', as Theophylact exclaimed. 'She will cherish thee with motherly affection,' Cornelius à Lapide (1567–1637) imagines Jesus as saying to the beloved disciple. 'She will console and protect thee, and ask help for thee from her Son,' he continues. Again, this 'adoption arrangement' is, of course, touching in its care and humanity – and instantly recognizable as the bonds of human affection we naturally need and cherish.

But seeing this third last word merely as an 'adoption' scene perhaps underplays the wider significance of the *hour* of the cross in which this third last word is spoken. In other words, what does this third last word have to say to us other than that we should in some general sense care for the needs of others?

On the other hand, as Christians further contemplated over the centuries this third last word, they often lent to it complex and abstract meanings. In many readings, Mary becomes the 'mother' of the Church, symbolized by the 'beloved disciple'. As the one whom Jesus addresses as 'woman', Mary stands as a 'second Eve' for a new humanity that finds its birth in the Church. Others read that Mary and the beloved disciple in this third last word are symbols of the Jewish and Gentile worlds, now united in Christ. In these kinds of readings of the third last word, Mary and the beloved disciple become 'ideal representatives of the Christian faith', as one commentary phrases it. Something of the vulnerable humanity of the scene is perhaps lost here, replaced by fleshless ciphers. Once again, we might be left wondering. We might strain to see how such abstractions speak to us in our everyday reality.

We might best understand, then, what we might hear in this third last word as the *holding together of the particular and the universal*. The third last word is at once *intimate* and stands as a *sign of a new disruptive reality* which Christ also commands us to see as a radical reorientation of community.

'From that hour,' the Gospel of John records, 'the disciple took her into his own home.' We can translate this passage as 'because of that hour, he took her into his own'. This translation reveals the power of the cross as it stands against the powers that crucify. We do well to attend to these two phrases 'because of that hour' and 'took her into his own'. They give us sight of just how *radical* this third last word might be.

Because of that hour. In this third last word, we are called to see the cross as a crucible where a new family is forged in the fires of kinship through Christ. Jesus speaks a command to all to *see* a new way of being – and to respond to it. The weight of the moment represents an urgent ethical imperative. The moment of the cross, of this third last word, is the point of death wrought by religious and political forces. These forces atrophy human connectedness in the pursuit of preserving power. These forces emerge in different ways across history and in our own age – but they are always there. There are countless little crucifixions performed by these forces in all places and times.

In the critical moment of these crucifixions, Jesus calls us to attend to kinship because of that hour. This is not a vague sentiment. It is to be our reality. *Behold* – Jesus calls us to see through the terrible power of the cross as a form of state torture to destroy life and community. *Behold* – Jesus calls us to see his power on the cross to recreate life in community around him. The bonds of kinship we are impelled to see *because* of the hour of the cross are to be a reality that disrupts the world in which we live.

The hour of the cross represents a crisis. The word 'crisis' comes from a Greek term that means something like a 'decisive moment of judgement' – or even the 'turning point of a disease'. The beloved disciple sees that Jesus on the cross creates a new family. This new creation disrupts the hour of the cross in which the unholy alliance of power and religion seek to dominate and destroy all bonds of family and friendship. The third last word on the cross is a decisive turning point in a social disease of violence. It is the divine impulse towards remaking wholeness in community. It is the social aspect of salvation – a word that comes from a sense of 'healing'.

He took her into his own. Pope Benedict explains how this means more than that the beloved disciple takes Mary into his home. It describes how the beloved disciple 'received her into his inner life setting'. The beloved disciple takes Mary as his *mother*. She takes the disciple as her *son*. They have a new social reality in one another through Jesus. Seeing someone else as family – bound not by biology but by the blood of Christ – disrupts the sight of earthly violence wrought by human kingdoms. This new sight reverses the experience of Jesus recorded at the beginning of John's Gospel and now seen in its initial horror at this hour of the cross – 'he came *to what was his own*, and his own people did not accept him' (John 1.11). The sight of kinship interrupts the violent status quo and its terrible claims to power. The sight envisages a new creation predicated upon everyday belonging, intimacy and care, rather than discord, violence and oppression. In a small, domestic manner, it is an act of subversive defiance that speaks a new truth to power. The beloved disciple obeys without hesitation Jesus's command to behold. He takes Mary into his own. Such obedience defies the terrible power displayed on the cross at this hour.

What we see in this scene is something that holds together both a down-to-earth reality of human care and an ideal of new community being represented. Kinship involves recognizing the person in front of us as *family* because of the hour of the cross – the countless little crucifixions that people endure. Kinship means dealing with the actual flesh and blood needs of the person in front of us. It means welcoming them as they are pulled apart by supra-personal forces of evil in the world that crucify bonds of belonging. Jesus calls us to see and take these people into our own – into our inner life setting as our beloved. Kinship also involves wrestling with the wider significance of that sight and hour. Kinship disrupts the distorting violence of the world in which we live. Kinship entails seeing and striving above all else for an alternative, preferred future – for the *kin-dom of God* articulated by Ada María Isasi-Díaz in our previous meditation.

That non-violent, healing, hospitable *kin-dom* of God puts a question mark against the world. The New Atheists make Christians hear that this third last word also places a question mark against religious communities too. In the antiseptic light of this third last word, history accuses Christian communities of the worst of crimes, a million crucifixions extending far beyond Golgotha. Christian communities have all too often failed to stand as the faithful four at the foot of the cross. Rather, they stand as images of the four Roman soldiers. Like those soldiers, Christian communities have and can crucify all sense of someone's humanity. They fail to behold kinship. They exclude, dominate, persecute and revile anyone and anything that threatens their beliefs or status. They even *kill*. Christian communities traumatize victims and their circles of care and support. Christianity's vile and violent history of religious persecution, gender discrimination, homophobia and racism – to name just a few sins – witnesses against the Church being anything like a social ethic. Rather, history testifies to Christian communities being a social disease as much as a virtue – a series of *failures to behold kinship*.

The third last word *chastens* the claims that Christian communities might want to make about themselves. It calls them to remember the constant and ongoing need to be disrupted by Jesus's command to *behold*. It is a crisis – a decisive moment of judgement – for how Christian communities see themselves, and whether they see others as Jesus commands. This third last word demands they attend to the constant need to repent and to let grace disrupt their sight. This will not, of course, answer any searching questions about the reasonableness of religious belief, such as posed by New Atheism. But it might lend greater authenticity to Christian communities and the consonance between their message and their lived reality. It might make them more capable of self-awareness and self-critique as Christ calls them to *behold*. As Mike Higton puts it, Christian discipleship invites two journeys, 'a journey deeper into the gift of God's love in Jesus Christ, and at the same time a journey out into the world'. Jesus draws us into kinship with him – and one another. The hour of the cross turns Christian discipleship, as Higton expresses it, 'towards the cries of those who suffer, including the cries of those injured, marginalized, erased, ignored, or forced into passivity', not only by the world but also 'by the existing patterns of the church's life'.

To get a sense of what all this might mean, the final word on this third last word best belongs to the African American womanist theologian, Kelly Brown Douglas.

In 2015, Brown Douglas published *Stand your Ground: Black Bodies and the Justice of God.* The book responded to the killing in 2012 of Trayvon Martin, an unarmed 17-year-old African American pupil. The person who killed Trayvon – George Zimmerman – was acquitted of murder after appealing to the controversial 'stand your ground' law that permits people to use lethal force in self-defence. Most studies indicate that 'stand your ground' laws lead to a disproportionate number of black deaths. They also show that the legal justice system disproportionately favours white people who appeal to 'stand your ground' laws as part of their legal defence against prosecution for murder. Brown Douglas points to white Christianity's historic complicity in such racism – and so to its complicity in deaths of people like Trayvon. She charts how white Christianity helped to construct blackness as 'sin' and 'threat', while at the same time casting whiteness as 'sacred' and 'safe'. Brown Douglas contends that the stand-your-ground culture has been most aggressive after every historical period in which new 'rights' were extended to African Americans, for example after emancipation, the civil rights era and the election of the first black president. When the structural power of 'whiteness' feels threatened, it exerts its power to crucify 'blackness'. 'Stand your ground' is just the latest iteration of how religious communities – in this case, white Christianity – help create systemic systems of violent oppression.

Brown Douglas turns back to the cross in this hour. Like we have seen in this third last word, the cross presents two sights for her. 'The cross,' Brown Douglas writes, 'reflects the lengths that unscrupulous power will go to sustain itself.' When we see the cross, we see 'the power that denigrates human bodies, destroys life, and preys on the most vulnerable in society'. 'There is no doubt,' she continues, 'that the guns of stand-your-ground culture are today's crosses.' Brown Douglas reminds us, however, that the cross invites another view that disrupts this first sight. 'Ironically,' Brown Douglas points out, 'the power that attempts to destroy Jesus on the cross is actually itself destroyed by the cross'. This 'death-negating, life-giving' and 'non-violent' way of being refuses that violent power has the final word. It opens a whole new way of being in community. That new way of being does not deny the reality of violence. It casts its critical gaze against it, wherever it exists in the world, including within religious communities. But it also represents a *new* sight to behold – that of resurrection. As Brown Douglas puts it, the power of God 'conquers death by resurrecting life'.

The third last word on the cross demands, then, that we open our eyes to behold kinship and strive for the kin-dom of God as the resurrection of life together. Whether we dare to behold this vision remains for us to respond.

4

'WHY?'

At three o'clock Jesus cried out with a loud voice, 'Eloi, Eloi, lema sabachthani?' which means, 'My God, my God, why have you forsaken me?' When some of the bystanders heard it, they said, 'Listen, he is calling for Elijah.' And someone ran, filled a sponge with sour wine, put it on a stick, and gave it to him to drink, saying, 'Wait, let us see whether Elijah will come to take him down.' Then Jesus gave a loud cry and breathed his last.

Mark 15.34–7 (compare Matthew 27.45–54)

Why should I respect a capricious, mean-minded, stupid God who creates a world which is so full of injustice and pain?

Stephen Fry

The so-called 'problem of evil' ought to be acknowledged as completely legitimate and as utterly unanswerable.

Karen Kilby

Jesus Christ is not a quick answer. If Jesus Christ is the answer, he is the answer in the way portrayed in crucifixion.

Kosuke Koyama (1929–2009)

This fourth last word is the *only* last word from the cross mentioned in *two* Gospels, namely those of Mark and Matthew. In both Mark and Matthew, Jesus repeats the fourth last word *twice* – once where the words he cries out are reported verbatim, but presumably again with his final shout before he dies. As such, the fourth last word might be said to be the *word of last words*.

That this fourth last word is doubly recorded and doubly spoken makes it carry a special significance. But as we hear Jesus cry out to God, what he says strikes us as shocking, even scandalous. It is, after all, a stumbling block – Jesus here seems *to doubt God*. The fourth last word is often called the 'cry of dereliction' as a result. Jesus takes the words that open Psalm 22 and makes them his own – '*My God, my God, why have you forsaken me?*' As he draws near to death, Jesus feels *godforsaken*. Amidst all the horrors of his crucifixion, the sense that his God has absconded and refuses comfort or help remains perhaps the *cruellest* moment of all. Jesus's whole life has been directed to the God he has intimately called 'Abba, Father' (Mark 14.36). This heavenly Father declared Jesus as his 'Beloved with whom I am well pleased' (Mark 1.11; Matthew 3.17). Now, God seems to be absent, silent, a cold void – and at the very moment that Jesus needs God the most.

The phrase 'Jesus cried out with a loud voice' might better be translated as 'screamed'. *Screamed* – Jesus feels an anguish in the hollow of his soul which cuts deeper and more keenly than the mortal wounds his body experiences. The cross that kills him is godlessness – a world without God. As Fleming Rutledge puts it, this fourth last word 'brings the *irreligiousness* of the cross into sharp focus'. No wonder that Jesus *doubts* God on the cross. No wonder that, as he 'breathes his last', 'the curtain of the temple was torn in two...the earth shook, and the rocks were split' (Matthew 27.51). The word of all last words screams a question to God – *why?*

This fourth last word is one that Christian readers have long felt discomforted by and sought to explain away. The early Church explained the cry of dereliction simply as a messianic fulfilment of Psalm 22. They interpreted what Jesus screams on the cross through the lens of their commitment that he was fully divine and fully human. Any doubt that Jesus expresses must only pertain to his human nature, and not to his divinity, for only that would seem to make sense. Ambrose of Milan (c. 339–397) wrote that 'it is not his divinity that doubts, but his human soul'. Augustine of Hippo (354–430) similarly exclaimed that Jesus here speaks with 'the voice of human weakness' and the 'speech of human infirmity' when faced with an apparent lack of divine consolation.

Later in the Christian tradition, others argued that it was *necessary* for Christ in his humanity to feel abandoned. John Calvin (1509–1564) thought, for example, that Jesus had to feel the utter alienation of the cross so that he might satisfy God's anger at our sinfulness. Calvin interpreted this fourth last word in the context of the Apostles' Creed that describes how Jesus 'descended into hell'. The descent into hell means, Calvin wrote, 'that [Jesus] had been afflicted by God, and felt the dread and severity of divine judgement, in order to intercede with God's wrath and make satisfaction to his justice in our name'. In other words, Jesus substitutes himself *for* us and takes a punishment due *to* us. He bears the full weight of God's wrath *in our place*. He descends into the hell of utter alienation from God in order to intercede for us. As such, Calvin continued that Jesus 'experienced all the signs of a wrathful and avenging God, so as to be compelled to cry out in deep anguish, "My God, my God, why hast thou forsaken me?"' Yet, 'it is not to be understood that the Father was ever angry towards Jesus', Calvin mysteriously concludes, but rather that 'his divinity for a little while was concealed'.

Much modern biblical scholarship has a similar tendency to explain away the anguished doubt of Jesus in his dying moments. Some commentators argue that it makes no sense and shows no 'good news' if Jesus actually suffers the anguish of doubt on the cross. Instead, they often say, we ought to infer that Jesus refers to Psalm 22 to evoke the *whole* of the psalm in the minds of those who hear him. While Psalm 22 is a psalm of lament, they say, it also commends ultimate trust in God. As such, Jesus recognizes the anguish of human suffering in his cry of dereliction. Yet, Jesus redirects it to God's fidelity. It's more our modern biblical illiteracy, the commentators say, that make us assume that Jesus feels godforsaken. The Gospel writers are disinterested, these commentators continue, in speculating about Jesus's emotional state on the cross. Rather, the Gospel writers are concerned to show how Jesus's death occurred according to the Scriptures. We indeed hear significant elements of Psalm 22 in the crucifixion of Jesus. 'All who see me mock at me,' the psalm complains, 'they make mouths at me, they shake their heads' (Psalm 22.7). 'You lay me in the dust of death,' the psalmist continues, 'they divide my clothes among themselves, and for my clothing they cast lots' (Psalm 22.15, 18). These are scenes recapitulated in the death of Jesus on the cross. As such, the commentators claim that Jesus quotes the psalm simply to undergird his messianic status and refer the hearer to trust in God's work of salvation.

We may feel uneasy, however, about these dismissive interpretive tendencies in the Christian tradition and modern biblical commentary. As one scholar, Raymond Brown, puts it, there seems 'no persuasive argument *against* attributing to the Jesus of Mark/Matthew the *literal* sentiment of feeling *forsaken* expressed in the psalm quote'. If we attend to the response in the Gospels of Mark and Matthew to the fourth last word, Brown seems right. In both Mark and Matthew, the whole of creation responds to Jesus's anguished sense of dereliction. Heaven and earth join him in lament, desolation and brokenness. The curtain of the Temple – a tough material that serves as a kind of door to God's presence – is torn in two from top to bottom. The solid earth quakes. Hard rocks split. The reaction of heaven and earth signals the rupture that the cross represents. All religious certainty, all stability and security, is torn, shook and split – even trust in God. In the hour of the cross – *because* of the hour of the cross – we are faced with what Luther called the 'Deus absconditus', meaning the 'hidden God'. At the cross, like Jesus in this fourth last word, we strain to find this hidden God. God has apparently fled from sight. God is absent from the troubles of the world.

This fourth last word presents a challenge, then, in and of itself. We move too quickly to look past it or to explain it away. This fourth last word poses without directly answering what is often called 'the problem of evil'. As we hear Jesus's cry of dereliction, we must attend to the dilemma of how to square claims about God's existence, power and goodness with the terrible experience of evil. This dilemma eddies around the scream of Jesus on the cross. The same dilemma floods before the cross and cascades beyond it. The 'problem of evil' is a curtain-tearing, rock-splitting, earth-quaking shockwave that pulses through every age.

The attempt to exonerate God of moral culpability for suffering occasioned by evil is known as 'theodicy'. That word comes from joining two Greek words that mean 'God' ('theos') and 'justice' ('dike'). Theodicy attempts to justify God when faced with the 'problem of evil'. The fourth last word poses the hard question about *where God is* in actual human suffering when God seems so utterly absent. It demands how God might be justified in the wake of the earthquake of desolation. It screams for an adequate theodicy to answer the desperate question *why?*

The 'problem of evil' has been posed by different philosophers and theologians across the centuries. Perhaps its most famous modern summary was given by the Scottish philosopher, David Hume (1711–1776). While he never directly mentions it, Hume's writings on the problem of evil emerged within the wider cultural context of a very literal earthquake. On 1 November 1755, while people worshipped on the Feast of All Saints, a series of tremors devastated the city of Lisbon. Churches were unable to withstand the seismic shock. Across the city, many collapsed, killing or injuring thousands of worshippers. Final estimates of the number of deaths varied, but casualties in the city alone were probably anywhere up to 50,000 – around one in four of the population. The Lisbon earthquake was one of the worst natural disasters on historical record. In the aftershock, people struggled how to make sense of the disaster. Some Christians spuriously claimed it must be God's judgement on the sins of the people of Lisbon. Others, such as the French philosopher Voltaire (1694–1778), questioned how any such event could be part of a providentially ordered world designed by a benevolent deity. As Voltaire saw it, after Lisbon it was impossible to think this was 'the best of all possible worlds' as the German philosopher Gottfried Leibniz (1646–1716) had argued. Across Europe, the Lisbon earthquake shook confidence in the ability to reconcile God and evil – or seemed only to leave the unpalatable and pastorally reckless option of attributing the blame for natural disasters on their victims. Today, we continue to stand in the same dilemma. We need only look to responses to the tsunami that ravaged South Asia in 2004, or the earthquake that devastated Haiti in 2010, to see contemporary parallels to Lisbon.

The earthquake that shook Lisbon also shook the moral imagination of the modern western world. It gave a common focal point to the 'problem of evil' that still haunts us today. As he lived in the aftermath of Lisbon, David Hume helps us to tease out the layers of this ancient but still pressing 'problem of evil' in a focused way. To explain the 'problem of evil', Hume borrowed from the ancient Greek philosopher, Epicurus. 'Epicurus's old questions are yet to be answered,' Hume wrote. For Epicurus, there were three baffling questions and problems about God and evil – sometimes called the Epicurean trilemma. Hume begins with the first old question: 'Is God willing to prevent evil, but not able?' If so, Hume avers, 'then he is impotent'. Hume then wonders about Epicurus's second old question: 'Is God able, but not willing [to prevent evil]?' If so, 'then he is malevolent'. Finally, Hume follows Epicurus's third old question and asks: 'Is God both able and willing [to prevent evil]?' Hume then ponders, 'whence then is evil?'

The Epicurean trilemma developed by Hume shows how difficult it is to exonerate God from the 'problem of evil'. We assert the intrinsic goodness and power of God over all things. Yet, evil and suffering are more than readily observable in the world. So, it seems as if we are trapped. Either God must not really exist, be powerless, wicked or remain an inscrutable mystery. The 'problem of evil', then, is both *logical* and *evidential*. On a logical level, it questions whether we can reconcile an all-loving, all-powerful God with the experience of evil. On an evidential level, it questions whether we can believe that God even exists given that we experience evil in manifold forms.

We still live in the aftermath of Lisbon and the ancient 'problem of evil' as laid out by Hume. Modern wars, genocides, famine and ecological devastation are just some of the large-scale moral atrocities and natural terrors that pose time and again the same 'problem of evil'. But the 'banality of evil' on an everyday level disrupts our experience of the world too. Natural evils like ill health or pestilence, and moral evils like cruelty and broken relationships, happen every day in every life and in every place. Some individuals or small groups face unspeakable horrors in their lives, such as abuse, exploitation, terrible physical suffering and the like. As Martin Luther King Jr (1929–1968) wrote, 'there is hardly anything more obvious than the fact that evil is present in the universe. It projects its nagging, prehensile tentacles into every level of human existence.'

Whatever the source that provokes the 'problem of evil' for us, life makes us question our goodness, the goodness of the world, or God's goodness when we are faced with what Martin Luther King calls the 'stark, grim, and colossal reality' of evil. The 'problem of evil' is one asked every day, sometimes in 'sighs too deep for words' (Romans 8.26). At moments in our lives, faced with the unimaginable evils suffered by others or by ourselves, we may want to scream like Jesus on the cross in his fourth last word, *My God, my God, why have you forsaken me?* Little wonder that for many, evil proves that God does not exist – or if God does exist, then God is unworthy of worship. The British comedian Stephen Fry captured this understandable animus well in a television interview when he was challenged about why he was an atheist. 'Why should I respect,' Fry demanded, 'a capricious, mean-minded, stupid God who creates a world which is so full of injustice and pain?' We might join Fry's anger in asking *why?*

Just as it has done with the fourth last word, Christian tradition has tried in various ways over the centuries to soften the challenge of the dilemma posed by the 'problem of evil'. As with interpretations of the fourth last word, these attempts remain uneasy and unsatisfactory. For example, some Christian thinkers have followed the early church thinker Irenaeus (c. 130–202) and argued that people can only morally develop because of experiencing evil, sometimes known as a 'soul making theodicy'. As such, experiencing evil can be said to be part of God's providential ordering of all things for a greater good. The idea that God permits evil for a greater good is a hard sell. As people suffer the devastating consequences of evil, it hardly seems right to claim it is simply for some greater purpose or end. Other Christians follow Augustine of Hippo (354–430) and locate evil in the misuse of human freedom. We are free to choose good or evil. As such, we bear the moral responsibility for our poor choices. While this gets God 'off the hook' for causing moral evil, it fails to explain why God permits such abuse of freedom at all. In turn, other modern thinkers let go of certain divine attributes such as omnipotence to try to dissolve the 'problem of evil' and acquit God. By this account, God's power is limited in some way and cannot prevent evil from happening. Nevertheless, God desires for things to be otherwise. God tries to persuade or lure creation to goodness. God does what God can under these conditions. Whether we can find this modern account of God and evil satisfying or appealing remains contestable.

Whatever line is taken, such varied Christian attempts to answer the 'problem of evil' are rarely, if ever, capable of being proclaimed to people as they experience evil. To assert a one-size-fits-all answer to the 'problem of evil' proves pastorally insensitive, crude and unhelpful. It rides roughshod over individual instances of human suffering for the sake of some abstract, totalizing and yet ultimately inadequate answer. As Rowan Williams, the former Archbishop of Canterbury, puts it, it remains 'more religiously imperative to be worried by evil than to put it into a satisfactory theoretical context'. Indeed, Williams reminds us that being worried by evil keeps 'obstinately open the perspective of the sufferer'. Williams accordingly questions 'who' a theodicy is for – and if it is not for the sufferer, then 'how can it fail to evade, to evade not only humanity, but divinity as well?'

The cry of desolation in the fourth last word demands a subtler response to the 'problem of evil'. Once again, the *diagnosis* of the 'problem of evil' is correct – it seems impossible to reconcile a loving God with the reality of suffering. Yet, Jesus's fourth last word questions the *terms* of the 'problem of evil' itself. Hume and the modern world developed the 'problem of evil' in abstract terms divorced from any substantial content. The meaning of 'God', 'goodness', 'power' and 'evil' have no flesh on them. They are taken as rather thin terms that evoke only a vague sense of who God is and what we mean by goodness and evil. As the Catholic theologian Karen Kilby explains, the classical 'problem of evil' remains 'detached from traditional patterns of Christian thinking about God'. We need to put flesh on the bone before even attempting to respond to the 'problem of evil'.

In contrast, the Christian faith invokes a complex scriptural story, a tradition and a set of practices. These stories, traditions and practices flesh out who 'God' is and what it means for God to be 'good' and 'powerful'. They shape how Christians experience God and how they might navigate the joys and trials of life in contemplation, prayer and service. These stories, traditions and practices cast 'evil' as an unnatural and alien intrusion into God's good creation. As the Swiss theologian Karl Barth (1886–1968) puts it, evil is 'necessarily incomprehensible and inexplicable to us as human beings'. For Barth, we cannot render evil as intelligible. 'Evil' represents an irrational and menacing opposition to goodness itself – it is what Barth calls the 'nothingness' vehemently opposed to God and God's creation. Just as Jesus reveals who God is, so too does his cross unveil the utter and incomprehensible nihilism of evil.

The limits of modern attempts to answer the 'problem of evil' mean we must reframe how we approach the 'why' question screamed by Jesus in the fourth last word. The only legitimate Christian response is to return to Christian narratives, traditions and practices to reorient themselves. This return fleshes out who God is and how to live in the experience of goodness and evil alike. In other words, we must return to the fourth last word on the cross to revisit the 'problem of evil' in a different vein.

In the fourth last word, Jesus gets no logical or evidential answer from God or anyone to his screamed question *why*? Neither should we think he expected one. God's silence says less about God than it does about our human inability to comprehend the desolation of evil. As Karen Kilby puts it, 'the so-called "problem of evil" ought to be acknowledged as completely legitimate and as utterly unanswerable'. When faced with suffering, we are right to demand an answer to the question *why*? But in the absence of an answer that can completely satisfy us, the real questions become practical ones, rather than logical or evidential quandaries. Like Christ's cry of dereliction, we must learn to live in the doubt occasioned by evil. The experience of evil provokes psychological reactions like the cataclysmic responses of the earth felt and seen as Jesus gives his cry of dereliction. As we experience evil, it rips apart our religious certainty, shakes our foundations and splits our understanding. We have valid but insoluble questions. We are left with the practical question of *survival* – as Ezekiel phrases it, 'how then can we live?' (Ezekiel 33.10).

Jesus's fourth last word expresses a very human experience of evil and demand for understanding. The cross represents all the worst impulses of humanity brought to bear on Jesus. Human history is replete, of course, with millions of crucifixions of various kinds before and after Christ's cross. In the fourth last word, we hear the cry of all humanity spoken on the lips of Jesus in the words of Psalm 22. We hear it taken into the heart of God– *My God, my God, why have you forsaken me?*

This fourth last word also carries, then, divine freight into the broader context of Jesus's life and resurrection. Jesus has lived a life 'full of grace and truth' (John 1.14) in the presence of the goodness of God. He has tasted the sweetness of that goodness. Now, in this fourth last word, Jesus experiences the painful absence of that goodness – he feels godforsaken and the horror of godlessness. As he screams '*why?*' on the cross, Jesus does not dispassionately pose the Epicurean trilemma as delineated by Hume. Rather, Jesus poses the questions given by what are sometimes known as 'practical theodicies'. More practically oriented theodicies begin with questions about *where to locate God* and *what we ought to do* when faced with actual human suffering. This approach worries less (or at least, not in the first instance) about theoretical responses to the logical and evidential 'problem of evil'. It does not begin with the issue of how to square divine attributes like omnipotence and omnibenevolence with the experience of evil. It does not begin with questions about whether God exists because of natural and moral evils. Rather, a more practically oriented theodicy asks: *how can we retain trust in God's goodness, especially when God seems so utterly absent as we experience evil?* It demands: *how do we respond to the suffering person before us?* It queries: *how can we survive evil?* These are the 'problems of evil' for Jesus on the cross in this last fourth word – and perhaps they ought to be ours too.

The biblical commentators on the fourth last word are half-right, then. Jesus surely does assume biblical literacy when he screams the opening words of Psalm 22. The biblical commentators assume that as Jesus recalls Psalm 22 as he dies, he implies we should skip straight from his apparent suffering to trust in God. 'In you our ancestors trusted,' the psalmist declares, 'they trusted, and you delivered them.' Despite apparent absence and silence, the psalmist proclaims that God 'did not hide his face from me, but heard when I cried to him' (Psalm 22.24). 'I will tell of your name to my brothers and sisters,' the psalmist rejoices, 'in the midst of the congregation I will praise you' (Psalm 22.22). Of course, for Christians Jesus defeats the cross in the resurrection, along with all the deadly powers it represents. Yet, as we have seen, we can't so easily or quickly slide past Jesus's suffering and doubt. Neither can we do so when faced with any human suffering and the doubt that attends it. To do so would be inauthentic to the cross itself as it contains in a microcosm both God and humanity. Instead, Jesus's fourth last word evokes both registers of Psalm 22 – that of dereliction and absence, and that of joy and presence. It holds these registers together as an uncomfortable and uneasy dissonance that resonates with how we experience God, evil and suffering.

In short, the fourth last word holds the tension between
two kinds of certainty that seem to point to very different
realities. We have one reality ripped, shaken and split by our
experience of evil. *My God, my God, why have you forsaken me?*
We also have another reality born of having tasted God's
goodness. *In the midst of the congregations, I will praise you.*

To help us appreciate what I mean by these two kinds of
certainty, we can draw upon a helpful distinction made by
the medieval scholastic, Thomas Aquinas (1225–1274), and
picked up by an Elizabethan divine, Richard Hooker (1554–
1600) in relation to the experience of suffering. Aquinas
distinguished between the 'certainty of evidence' and the
'certainty of adherence'. Hooker used this distinction to
hold the tension between the contrary experiences of God's
goodness and the doubt occasioned by evil. On the one hand,
since God transcends creation, there is no physical evidence
that directly proves that God exists. As we are faced with
suffering, then, we have good reason to *doubt* God. We lack
the *certainty of evidence* to secure our sense that God is good,
cares or even exists. We understandably cry out with Jesus
on the cross *My God, my God, why have you forsaken me?* Yet,
this is not the whole story as we suffer. Christians have also
experienced God's goodness. This experience of goodness
evokes a *certainty of adherence* by which hearts cling to God
in trust through adversity. Hooker described this certainty
of adherence in this way: 'having once truly tasted [God's]
heavenly sweetness, all the world is not able to remove
someone from it'. Hooker continues how such a person
'strives to hope even against hope, to believe against all reason
of believing' because 'this lesson remains forever imprinted,

that it is *good for me to cleave to God* '. Christians hold together these two registers – those of doubt and of trust – every time they hear the stories of salvation, pray, worship and serve. The Christian narratives, traditions and practices are there to orient the believer in the complex and varied emotional ecosystem of being fully human before God.

The fourth last word, then, points towards how we might *survive* the horrors of evil. It does not – and it cannot – explain away the 'problem of evil'. It redirects how we might frame suffering in a way that refuses evil the *only* or *last* word. The cross gives us a theodicy of *protest* against the nihilism of evil. The last words of Christ provide a *practical* theodicy to place our suffering into a wider, more complex, and even indignantly hopeful story.

The final word on this fourth last word perhaps best belongs, then, to one of the greatest Japanese theologians of the twentieth century, Kosuke Koyama. Popularly known as Ko, much of his work revolved around how the cross is the archetypal symbol of suffering. For Ko, the cross acts as the key to unlock all theological reflection on the character of God and humanity. We must begin with the theology of the cross, or what the German Reformer Martin Luther called the *theologia crucis*. We cannot short-circuit the cross to get to the glory of the resurrection, or what Luther called the *theologia gloriae*. Theology must be able to speak this fourth last word on its own terms – or it has nothing to say at all. The fourth last word calls us to attend to suffering, rather than explain it away. The fourth last word asks us to be *worried* by what happens on Good Friday. We are to stand close to all and every little crucifixion in our communities. We are to show *compassion*, a word that literally means to 'suffer with'. As Ko puts it, if we have any response at all, 'Jesus Christ is not a quick answer.' Indeed, 'if Jesus Christ is the answer, he is the answer in the way portrayed in crucifixion'. The fourth last word directs us not so much to an answer to the question *why*, but to a focused concern on *what* we will do when faced with actual human suffering – and how we might survive.

5

'THIRST'

After this, when Jesus knew that all was now finished, he said (in order to fulfil the scripture), 'I am thirsty.'

John 19.28

If we examine the...genesis of religious ideas...[we find] they are illusions, fulfilling the oldest, most powerful, most pressing desires of the human race; the secret of their strength is the strength of those desires.

Sigmund Freud (1856–1939)

Both the cross and the lynching tree represented the worst in human beings and at the same time 'an unquenchable....thirst' for life that refuses to let the worst determine our final meaning.

James Cone (1938–2018)

The fifth last word is the *shortest* of the seven last words. It is also one with the *densest* of meanings. It is a last word about *desire*. It sounds direct and simple: *I am thirsty*. That Jesus physically desires water remains unsurprising at this late stage in his crucifixion. After being bound, dragged, caged, starved, beaten, slashed, berated, marched, mauled and crucified, Jesus thirsts. His prolonged torture has caused severe dehydration. Blood loss, sweat, shock, acidosis and slow suffocation have cracked his lips and parched his throat like a desert. Yet, the thirst in this fifth last word also exceeds physical desire. In the Scriptures, thirst describes spiritual desire too. In Hebrew, the word 'nephesh' means 'soul', the inner being of a person. But 'nephesh' can also mean 'thirst'. The Scriptures often depict each human being as a living thirst for God. 'My soul thirsts for God, for the living God,' says the psalmist (Psalm 42.2; compare Psalm 63.1 and Psalm 143.6). The prophet Isaiah exhorts people to find abundant life in God, inviting 'everyone who thirsts, [to] come to the waters' (Isaiah 55.1). God assures that spiritual desires will be fulfilled. 'Blessed are those who hunger and thirst for righteousness,' Jesus teaches, 'for they will be filled' (Matthew 5.6). In this fifth last word, then, thirst and desire coincide. Jesus thirsts for physical water to quench his throat. He also thirsts for *righteousness*, meaning for *right relations* to be remade – he thirsts for the fullness of life in God.

John's Gospel is the only one to record the fifth last word, and it does so with tortured irony. The one who cries out 'I am thirsty' has also been the one who has previously said 'let anyone who is thirsty come to me' (John 7.37).

In John's Gospel, Jesus casts himself as the 'living water' – an image used by the prophet Jeremiah to describe God (Jeremiah 2.13, 17.13). 'Those who drink of the water that I will give,' Jesus says, 'will never be thirsty.' 'The water that I will give,' Jesus continues, 'will become in them a spring of water gushing up to eternal life' (John 4.14). Jesus is the living water who quenches spiritual thirst for righteousness, for the restoring of right relations. Now, we see this 'living water' apparently dried up on the cross. The crucifixion is a spiritual drought. The cross is an arid desolation that parches souls as well as bodies. The cross arrests us with the sight of brokenness – not merely of broken bodies and souls, but of broken communities. The cross is *unrighteousness*. 'For our sake,' writes St Paul, God made Jesus 'to be sin who knew no sin, so that in him we might become the righteousness of God' (2 Corinthians 5.25). In this crucifixion scene, the living water now cries out *I am thirsty*. His thirst is not just physical. As he dies, Jesus thirsts for us. In Christ, we hear God's desire for us. We see God's righteousness clash with unrighteousness. In Christ, we hear that God still yearns for us. We hear God's longing to quench our spiritual thirst with the living waters of a new way of being.

In this fifth last word, then, John's Gospel carefully holds together the physical reality of tortured thirst with the defiant quenching of spiritual thirst. Jesus speaks this fifth last word when he knew that 'all was finished'. The original Greek word for 'finished' ('tetelestai') suggests a sense of end, completion or fulfilment. The whole of Jesus's life has led to this moment. We are right to pity the tortured thirst that Jesus experiences in the agony of the cross. The cross figures forth the brutal, barren and scorched realities of human brokenness, and the terrible thirst for righteousness it produces. Yet, this fifth last word also unveils a disruptive spiritual reality of ultimate significance. The cross represents the saving power of God that interrupts the powers that crucify people and relationships. 'I lay down my life for my sheep,' Jesus says, 'I have power to lay it down, and I have power to take it up again. I have received this command from my Father' (John 10.15, 18). In this fifth last word, Jesus speaks *defiantly* of the divine prospect of resurrection at the very moment of death.

When Jesus knew that all was now finished. The moment of this fifth last word gives it dense significance. The word 'finished' does not mean to suggest that Jesus resigns himself to stoic defeat and death. The original Greek word ('tetelestai') translated as 'finished' is in what is known as the perfect tense. We don't have quite the same tense in English, making it hard to grasp the significance of the word. In the perfect tense, something has both happened and will continue to happen. The perfect tense is both *punctiliar* (in the sense that something has been done) and *linear* (in the sense of an action that shapes every ongoing moment). Teasing out this double aspect of the perfect tense of the word 'finished' helps unpack the disruptive kernel of this shortest of last words. As Jesus pants 'I am thirsty' in the horror of the cross, he defiantly proclaims something about how human and divine yearning coincides, and he promises a new way in that thirst.

Finished: Jesus has completed the messianic prophecies through the manner of his death. Seeing that the time is right, Jesus cries 'I am thirsty' to indicate the work of the cross completes that which was foretold by the Scriptures. This fifth last word recalls Psalm 22: 'my mouth is dried up like a potsherd, and my tongue sticks to my jaws; you lay me in the dust of death' (Psalm 22.15). As the soldiers offer Jesus sour wine in response to his thirst, we hear Psalm 69 now fulfilled: 'for my thirst they gave me vinegar to drink' (Psalm 69.21). In this moment, the saving work promised by God is completed. *We see who Jesus is* – namely, the Chosen One of God. In that sight, *we know God's love for us*.

Finished: the perfect tense also carries a sense that 'it will continue to be completed'. Jesus sees that righteousness – the righting of relations – will continue to be completed in us. Righteousness will unfold in us *because of this hour*. Jesus's thirst has explosive power to transform us. *I am thirsty* – Jesus speaks of his thirst *for us*. 'Come to me,' Jesus says, 'all you that are weary and are carrying heavy burdens, and I will give you rest' (Matthew 11.28). The Roman Catholic *Catechism* writes that Jesus's thirst 'arises from the depths of God's desire for us'. Augustine of Hippo (354–430) puts it even more elegantly: *God thirsts to be thirsted for*. Jesus's thirst shows God's utter and radical commitment to us. Even as God faces the worst impulses brought to focus on Jesus on the cross, God still desires us. 'God proves his love for us,' St Paul writes, 'in that while we were still sinners, Christ died for us' (Romans 5.8). Pope Francis reflected in a Good Friday sermon in 2015 about this fifth last word in a similar manner. 'In your thirst, Lord,' pondered Francis, 'we see the thirst of your merciful Father who wanted through you to embrace, forgive, and save all of humanity.' This thirsty God promises to quench our spiritual thirst for right relations through Christ as the 'living water'. In God's desire for us – and in the living water of the Christ – we have the promise and sight of a new way of being.

The thirst of this fifth last word, then, above all else signals the mutual burning desire between human souls and God. This fifth last word couches faith in terms of an innate spiritual longing that orients us godward. 'Our hearts are restless,' prayed St Augustine to God, 'until they rest in you.' As Jesus speaks this fifth last word, he expresses the ongoing and dynamic desire of God for us – and vice versa. This mutual spiritual thirst unfolds in the messiness of human lives and communities. It is the slow unfurling of God in history. God quenches both the divine thirst for us and our thirst for God. 'For waters shall break forth in the wilderness,' prophesies Isaiah, 'and streams in the desert; the burning sand shall become a pool, and the thirsty ground springs of water' (Isaiah 35.6–7).

This fifth last word speaks to us still of how God quenches the deepest of human longing. God meets our desire, our thirst, with God's own fierce desire to make all things new. Little wonder that in the vision of the end of time in the Book of Revelation, we hear Jesus repeat what he first declared in his earthly ministry. 'It is done!', Jesus proclaims in the Book of Revelation. 'To the thirsty,' he promises, 'I will give water as a gift from the spring of the water of life' (Revelation

21.6). At the end of all time, God in Christ satiates our thirst with abundant waters for the fullness of life together. But that time has already begun to break into the world through the fifth last word on the cross. 'I am thirsty' is our cry to God. 'I am thirsty' is God's cry to us. In this fifth last word, Christ invites us to quench all thirst: 'let everyone who is thirsty come. Let anyone who wishes take the water of life as a gift' (Revelation 22.17).

Not everyone, however, might take at face value these religious claims about the desire for God. There are reasons to be *suspicious* of what this fifth last word seems to suggest about thirst and desire. We might wonder, for example, if we can accept the idea that we are constituted by a soul that desires God. We might question whether our desires truly reveal anything about God's existence or nature. We might rather query whether religious claims are illusory projections of human desires – or as Feuerbach put it, that 'theology is anthropology'. We might want to dig deeper to uncover what our desires might say *about us* rather than God. We might want to dare to know the subterranean truths of human desires – and the challenges they might pose for religion.

To delve into these doubts about desire, we can turn to the last of Paul Ricoeur's 'masters of suspicion', namely Sigmund Freud. Like Nietzsche and Marx, Freud sought to uncover the origin of religion – and indeed, Freud saw himself as following in Nietzsche's footsteps in this regard. For Nietzsche, the true origin of religion was conflict over power. For Marx, it was conflict over economic production. For Freud, the real origin of religion was the hidden workings of the human mind and its desires. Like the other two 'masters of suspicion', Freud's suspicious explanation aimed to liberate people from religion and for human autonomy. We can see the interweaving of psychology and religion in Freud's thought by turning to him and his work – and then turn to the challenge it poses as we consider the fifth last word on the cross.

Like the other masters of suspicion, Freud was an atheist with a religious background. He was born to Jewish parents in the Roman Catholic town of Freiberg, Moravia. Freud trained as a medic and then specialized in neuropathology. He spent most of his working life in Vienna, where he developed his therapeutic practice and psychological theories through the university there. Freud perhaps became best known for placing sex at the centre of his therapeutic work and psychological analysis of human nature. This account reduces, however, the revolutionary significance and ambition of his thought. In what became known as psychoanalysis, Freud looked to the whole of human life as the extension of often hidden psychological phenomena. Freud sought to unveil what was *really* going on in the world. This unveiling was *therapeutic*. Understanding the inner working and desires of our minds – our psychology – would help us understand *why* we act in the way we do, both as individuals and as societies. These psychological insights, Freud thought, would help us live more mature and healthier lives. As such, his entire psychoanalytical enterprise was to 'agitate the sleep of mankind' – to wake us up to our reality.

Religion did not escape the methodical gaze of Freud's psychoanalysis. Throughout his life, Freud explored the hidden psychological foundations of religion. He wrote numerous books on religion, including *Totem and Taboo* (1913), *Civilization and Its Discontents* (1930) and *Moses and Monotheism* (1939). Perhaps Freud's most popular work on religion, however, was *The Future of an Illusion*, published in 1927. Turning to this work, then, gives us a cipher to unlock the broad contours of Freud's suspicious explanation of religious desire.

The Future of an Illusion describes Freud's psychoanalytic interpretation of religion's origins, development and future. It unpacks what Freud sees as the hidden psychological dynamics that led to the cultural production of religion. For Freud, religion represents a 'universal neurosis', an 'illusion' that fulfils various psychological and social functions. He argues that science gives true explanations of human drives and social structures that will go beyond the neurotic limits of religion.

Having set these broad contours of *The Future of an Illusion*, we can examine in more detail Freud's critique of religion as a psychological phenomenon. We can chart how the ideas of *culture*, *neurosis*, *illusion* and *science* play interlocking parts in his suspicious explanation of religious desire. They will help cast religious beliefs as a psychological projection of the most basic human need for security in an uncertain world. They will offer an interpretive challenge to how we might view this fifth last word on the cross.

For Freud, psychoanalysis unveils not only the psychological condition of an individual but also the psychological make-up of entire *cultures*. As such, he first explores what we might mean by 'human culture'. For Freud, 'human culture' includes two aspects. First, it describes 'the knowledge and skills that humanity has acquired in order to control the forces of nature and obtain from it the goods that satisfy human needs'. Second, it describes 'all the institutions that are required to govern' human relations and the distribution of goods.

In both instances, 'human culture' has a psychological or 'mental' aspect to it as well as a 'material' function. 'Human culture' exists to secure what is materially required for survival and growth. It also exists to control human social relations. 'Human culture' must restrict individual desires as social groups pursue common goods and avoid descending into chaos. Such restrictions frustrate individual desires to protect social stability and harmonious relationships. What Freud calls 'civilization' accordingly rests on a dilemma. People need civilization ('human culture') for protection. Yet, people are subconsciously frustrated with social prohibitions on their individual drives. As such, 'human culture' produces 'mental assets' to compensate for the social privation of individual desires. These 'mental assets' are things like the food, art and technologies we associate with particular societies. They give a sense of belonging and pride in social identity that turn individuals 'from being enemies of culture to being upholders of culture'. We might think, for example, of the kinds of things that people associate with being English, American or South African as examples of 'mental assets'. These 'mental assets' make people in those societies willing to have their freedom limited in certain ways for the perceived value and status of those cultural identities.

For Freud, 'religion' represents one such 'mental asset'. Religion is a *product* of 'human culture' – once again the idea from Feuerbach that really 'theology is anthropology'. For Freud, 'the main function of culture...is to shield us against nature'. Since nature is dangerous and cruel, human beings create a kind of divine technology to ward off the terrors of nature, reconcile humankind to the cruelty of fate (especially death), and compensate them for sufferings and privations in this world. Religion as a 'mental asset' makes 'human helplessness bearable'. Religious belief also provides supposedly divine warrants for the social control and restriction of individual behaviours. The threat of eternal punishment – or the promised reward of heaven – motivates socially advantageous behaviours. Through a lengthy development, then, human societies produce the idea of a protective divine figure. This divine figure eventually becomes imaged as a 'Father', 'corresponding approximately to the end result in our present-day white Christian culture'.

Freud understands religion, then, as a 'universal neurosis'. For Freud, a 'neurosis' is an obsessional psychological adaptation to environmental threat or repressed trauma. While a 'neurosis' provides psychological coping mechanisms for these threats, they can inhibit mature human flourishing. Freud concedes that everyone is neurotic in certain ways, and not all neurotic behaviours cause harm. The neurotic who needs treatment, however, exhibits a debilitating inability to engage life in its fullness. Religious belief is one such debilitating neurosis. Therapy remains essential for such neurosis. 'A neurotic who is cured,' Freud wrote, 'has really become another man…he has become what he might have become at best under the most favourable conditions.'

As he considers religion as a 'universal neurosis', Freud queries 'why are [religious beliefs] held in such high esteem, and…what are they actually worth?' The prospect for religion seems bleak to Freud – and renders religious believers in need of therapy. He argues there is a 'very remarkable psychological problem' that religious beliefs which 'might be of the greatest significance' in fact 'have the feeblest authentication of all'. They seem to depend upon an appeal to religious authority, whether of our ancestors or of supposed divine revelation. This authority cannot be questioned – it is not open to rational scrutiny.

Freud argues that the inability of religion to show its reasonableness renders religion as an 'illusion'. Freud distinguishes an 'illusion' from a 'delusion'. A 'delusion' is utterly inconsistent with reality. It persists despite blatant contradiction. For example, we might think of the delusional person who believes he is the King of Denmark, although he is definitively not. In contrast, what Freud means by 'illusion' is something like the following: it is a belief that is likely incorrect, but which allows someone to believe that a wish has been (or will be) fulfilled. Freud gives the example of a middle-class girl who entertains the illusion that a prince will marry her. That might happen – but it's extremely unlikely and causes her to entertain all sorts of maladaptive fantasies. For Freud, 'armed with this information', we can see that religious beliefs are likewise 'all illusions, unverifiable, no one should be forced to regard them as true, to believe in them'. Indeed, compared with the illusion of the middle-class girl, the religious belief that 'the Messiah will come and establish a new golden age is far less likely' – so much so that the messianic belief borders upon delusion. Unveiling the 'psychical genesis of religious ideas', Freud writes, reveals in fact that 'they are illusions, fulfilling the oldest, most powerful, most pressing desires of the human race; the secret of their strength is the strength of those desires'. In other words, we can intelligibly grasp that behind religious desires and beliefs stands an understandable psychological neurosis – a kind of *wish-fulfilment* with no likely basis in reality.

For Freud, that religion is an 'illusion' makes it a *false consciousness*. This false consciousness needs therapeutic relief through the science of psychoanalysis. 'Scientific work,' he concludes, 'is the sole avenue that can lead to knowledge outside of ourselves.' 'In the long run,' Freud argues, 'nothing can withstand reason and experience.' Psychoanalysis allows people to outgrow the neuroses that inhibit them. As such, it can help people outgrow religion too. Psychoanalysis unmasks religion as an obsessional universal neurosis. Psychoanalysis allows people to reach greater maturity and confront reality as it is. 'Like the obsessional neurosis of children,' Freud wrote, religion 'arose out of the Oedipus complex, out of the relation to the father.' Now that psychoanalysis reveals the hidden origins of religion, individuals and societies can be freed from its psychological maladaptation. We can be freed for adult maturity in the world. 'A turning-away from religion,' Freud wrote, 'is bound to occur with the fatal inevitability of a process of growth.' Religion is a 'lost cause' – it represents an infantile neurosis that we must outgrow. Psychoanalysis allows us to understand our desires for what they are. Science promises rational development and progress for how we understand the world and our place in it. 'Our science', Freud concludes 'is not an illusion.' 'What would be an illusion,' he avers, 'would be to think we might obtain elsewhere that which science cannot give us.'

We will react differently to Freud. We may variously find ourselves uneasy with, or appreciative of, his psychological account of desire and religion. We may be persuaded by, or sceptical of, how he demolishes religious attempts to infer that God exists from the human longing for order and meaning amidst chaos and cruelty. Whatever our reaction, Freud brings to light an important insight about the complexity of human psychology in relation to religion. It remains very easy to accept at face value without any critical self-examination the spiritual desire that the fifth last word on the cross infers. As we face this fifth last word, we must face what really might be going on in our desires. The Harvard biologist William Morton Wheeler (1865–1937) celebrated Freud and other psychoanalysts for this reason. He lauded those like Freud who 'have had the courage to dig up the subconscious, that hotbed of all the egotism, greed, lust, pugnacity, cowardice, sloth, hate and envy which every single one of us carries about as his inheritance from the animal world'. That very human reality is one we cannot and should not avoid. Indeed, after Freud, we have to wrestle with the idea, as one contemporary scholar of religion affirms, that 'the right place to look for the origins and causes of religion must be in the minds that create (and continually recreate) it'.

Freud makes us face, then, the *uncomfortable* truth that religious talk about spiritual desire and thirst for another way of being does not represent the whole story. Freud's *diagnosis* remains insightful: the expression of religious desire hides what might be truly going on. All too often, religious belief might legitimate dark desires with catastrophic social consequences. Religious belief shapes how we view and understand the world, but also how we act in the world, for good and for ill. Religious belief legitimates the darkest acts of violence and oppression imaginable. We cannot forget that the cross is a symbol of the alliance of political and religious powers alike to kill that which threatens them. All too often, religious belief might inhibit us from seeing the world as it is, our place within that world, and the actions we ought to take. Religion may make us into the executor rather than the victim of crucifixion.

Freud's *prognosis*, however, seems more tenuous. It certainly remains *necessary* to plumb the psychological depths of desire – this is an act of honesty and self-awareness. Yet, it's not *sufficient* to say that this psychological account exhausts what's going on in human desires – or the positive role that spiritual desire might play in creating more authentic and mature human relationships in society. To be fair, Freud admits this possibility. It's why he does not deny the possibility that God might exist, or that religious beliefs might be true, however unlikely. Yet, we need to be suspicious – and that suspicion might just be a gift into great self-awareness and moral responsibility.

If we return to the fifth last word after Freud's critique of religion, we can see two signs that chasten us to have greater psychological self-awareness. We can see the *obsessional capacity* of desire for destructive illusion that runs perilously close to self-delusion. We can also see the *creative capacity* of desire to disrupt illusion and self-delusion.

To help us see these two signs, we can turn to the African American theologian, James Cone (1938–2018), one of the founders of what became known as 'Black Theology'. In 2011, Cone published *The Cross and the Lynching Tree*. In that book, he explored the racial intersections between the cross of Christ and the historical lynching of African Americans in the United States. Lynching was what Cone describes as a 'ritual celebration of white supremacy'. Lynching involved not only hanging but also 'burning, beating, dragging, and shooting – as well as torture, mutilation, and especially castration'. Lynching was used to remind African Americans 'of their inferiority and powerlessness'. It was the 'quintessential symbol of black oppression in America'. Cone then presses why white Christians haven't attended to the similarity between the lynching tree and the cross. He challenges why white Christians who lynched never noticed they took the violent role of those who murdered their non-violent and innocent Christ. Instead, the cross was 'a harmless, non-offensive ornament' that served as a status symbol for white holiness as it mercilessly lynched black people.

Cone argues that we must see the cross alongside the lynching tree to 'help us see Jesus in America in a new light'.

In *The Cross and the Lynching Tree*, Cone unveils how religious belief and desire can both *legitimate* oppression and *disrupt* that same violence.

At first, as we look both at the cross and the lynching tree, we see death and hear mortal thirst. On the cross, we see the deadly alliance of politics and religion as they desire power. On the lynching tree, we see the deadly alliance of race and privilege in pursuit of the same desire for power. As we turn from the cross to the lynching tree, we see and hear how the desire of white racism uses the cross to give an aura of holiness to the lethal heresy of white supremacy. Those who lynch are Christians. Yet, they fail to see any dissonance between the desires of their faith and the deadly desires of their hearts. The obsessional neurosis of white racism – and its perception that black people are racially inferior and dangerous – blinds them to where they truly stand in relation to the cross. They do not stand with the faithful four at the foot of the cross. They stand as Pilate, the mob, the religious authorities and the soldiers who crucify. White racism leads to destructive illusion that borders on delusion.

As we look and listen more closely, however, Cone argues that the same cross disrupts the racist desire of white supremacy made manifest on the lynching tree. The cross has a creative capacity to reform our desires. 'God took the evil of the cross and lynching tree,' Cone wrote, 'and transformed them both into the triumphant beauty of the divine.' The Gospel is 'a story about God's presence in Jesus's solidarity with the oppressed, which led to his death on the cross'. The resurrection of Christ gives oppressed people 'meaning beyond history, when such violence as slavery and lynching seemed to close off any future'. The cross gives us hope 'beyond tragedy'. 'Both the cross and the lynching tree,' Cone wrote, 'represented the worst in human beings and at the same time "an unquenchable...thirst" for life that refuses to let the worst determine our final meaning.' Or, as St Paul puts it, 'if we have been united with Jesus in a death like his, we will certainly be united with him in a resurrection like his' (Romans 6.5).

In short, Cone's complex reflection on the cross and the lynching tree show how desire and thirst meet in challenging ways in the fifth last word. *I am thirsty*. This last word unveils that the physical desires of the crucified are taken into the heart of God. It reveals that God desires a new way that interrupts crucifixion. Jesus *thirsts* for the oppressed, who themselves thirst for justice and righteousness, the righting of relations. Jesus suffers alongside the oppressed – shows *compassion* to them. As the living water awaiting resurrection, Jesus's thirst also critiques and defeats all the deadly powers of the world. His thirst is *our* thirst for God. His thirst is also God's thirst for us. Jesus's thirst then confronts us. Do our desires place us as the one who *causes* horrific thirst? Or do our deepest desires locate us as the one who gives living waters leading to eternal life?

Confronting this fifth last word with Freud and Cone, then, keeps us *honest* about ourselves and how our psychology shapes us. If we are to speak of human and divine longing, we must attend to all that we may desire. We must search our souls for the 'egotism, greed, lust, pugnacity, cowardice, sloth, hate and envy' that may shape our cravings. These make up who we are – and the horrors we can commit in the name of religion – just as much as those desires that drive us towards goodness and God. *I am thirsty*. As Jesus speaks this fifth last word, he questions *for what* we might thirst – and the next word will be ours.

6

'FINISHED'

A jar full of sour wine was standing there. So they put a sponge full of the wine on a branch of hyssop and held it to his mouth. When Jesus had received the wine, he said, 'It is finished.' Then he bowed his head and gave up his spirit.

John 19.29–30

Whichever way you look at it, theology has failed.

Marika Rose

In order to deny every kind of idolatry possible, a Christian must be every kind of atheist possible.

Denys Turner

The sixth last word on the cross is the last of three recorded in the Gospel of John. We have already reflected on the first two of these three last words: *Behold* and *I am thirsty*. In these two last words from John's Gospel, Jesus interrupts and disrupts what we see on the surface. He interrupts the violence that leads to the cross. On the cross, we see religion and politics join forces to protect their power. Crucifixion acts as their tool to oppress and destroy all that threatens their clout. Crucifixion destroys both those crucified and their communities. The cross causes a desperate thirst, for life and for right relations respectively. Jesus also disrupts the sense that this violent power has the final word. In Christ, we behold a new community spoken into being. In him, this new community drinks the living water that flows out of the parched cross to recreate right relations. These first two last words in John's Gospel defiantly turn upside down the brokenness we might otherwise see as an inevitable feature of the world. Against the grain of the cross, they speak a new way of being, a new creation, configured by kinship.

It is finished. The sixth last word likewise interrupts and disrupts what we initially see and hear on the cross. It interrupts and disrupts the patent sense of *failure* – that Christ and the kingdom of God he proclaimed has *failed* because he dies such a shameful death.

On the surface, the death of Jesus on the cross appears, of course, to be such a moment of *supreme failure*. As we have seen, crucifixion was abominable to Jewish and Roman political and religious sensibilities alike. The cross was what St Paul calls a 'scandal' (1 Corinthians 1.23). This word translates the Greek term 'skandalon', meaning 'stumbling block'. In the crucifixion, Jesus becomes a 'curse for us' (Galatians 3.13). In Jewish law, 'anyone hung on a tree is under God's curse' (Deuteronomy 21.22–3). Likewise, the Romans used crucifixion to punish the 'scum of the earth' – 'slaves, enemy soldiers, and those held in the highest contempt and lowest regard in society', as the womanist theologian Kelly Brown Douglas explains. For Jewish and Roman minds alike, the cross rendered as utterly foolish any claim that Jesus was a victorious messiah sent by God.

It is finished. This is not, however, a last word of resigned defeat or disaster. It is a defiant word. The sixth last word interrupts and disrupts the surface view of failure. The cross interrupts what we think truly measures power and success. We saw in the last chapter that the Greek word 'tetelestai' translated into English as 'finished' means something like 'completed', 'perfected', 'consummated' or 'fulfilled'. The final moment of Jesus's death presents him as completing, perfecting, consummating or fulfilling something. The cross is not a failure – but we still need to understand *what* is perfected on the cross and *why* the cross fulfils something.

The whole of John's Gospel gears itself to *what* is being 'finished' by Jesus on the cross and *why* the cross perfects the life and ministry of Christ. This sixth last word declares two beginnings found in John's Gospel to now be ended. The first beginning is from the opening of John's Gospel. Seeing the end on the cross of this beginning unveils *what* Christ fulfils. The second beginning is the start of Jesus's journey to the cross in that same Gospel. Seeing the end on the cross of this beginning reveals *why* the crucifixion manifests what St Paul calls 'the power of God' rather than failure (1 Corinthians 1.18). Let's return to each of these two beginnings in John's Gospel, then, to unpack the endings found on the cross.

It is finished. In the sixth last word, Jesus means he has fulfilled his original purpose as the divine 'Word [who] became flesh and lived among us' (John 1.14). The beginning of John's Gospel declares that Jesus came so that we can see and know God. 'No one has ever seen God,' writes the evangelist John – no one except Jesus, 'who is close to the Father's heart' and 'who has made him known' (John 1.18; compare John 6.46). 'The Father and I are one,' Jesus declares (John 10.30). In John's Gospel, Jesus constantly invokes God as his 'Father'. Jesus constantly invites people to know the love of the Father. The crucifixion fully discloses *who this God is*. 'God did not send the Son into the world to condemn the world,' Jesus says 'but in order that the world might be saved through him' (John 3.16). Through the cross, we see the 'power of God' to save us out of love (1 Corinthians 1.18). 'For God so loved the world,' Jesus teaches, 'that he gave his only Son, so that everyone who believes in him may not perish but may have eternal life' (John 3.15). On the cross, we see that 'God's weakness is stronger than human strength' (1 Corinthians 1.25). Jesus's death completely unveils the power of God's utter love for us. The cross completes Christ's purpose to disclose and manifest who God is. In the cross, we see perfectly how God faces the worst excesses of human evil – and still speaks love.

In this sixth last word, then, we are interrupted with the perfect sight of who God is – namely, that 'God is love' (1 John 4.8). God's love may seem weak, foolish and a failure when we see Christ's body broken on the cross. But the divine love that inhabits Jesus interrupts the horror of the crucifixion. God's love opens our eyes to see the 'power of God' in the crucified Christ. God's love disrupts the horror of the cross so that we see an alternative vision that can reshape how we understand who God is for us. Jesus on the cross becomes the 'horror-defeater', as the American theologian Marilyn McCord Adams (1943–2017) phrased it. Seeing the 'power of God' in Christ on the cross dissolves our inability to see the transcendent God who is love. It allows us perfectly to see the power of God's love as definitive, even against all the powers that oppose it.

It is finished. What the cross unveils about us is now perfected too. The sixth last word returns us to the beginning of the passion narrative in John's Gospel that describes the final days of Jesus's life. The completion of the passion narrative interrupts and disrupts what we see about ourselves. It explains why it is necessary for Christ to suffer and die on the cross. The cross allows us to behold who we might be, even as we see who we are in our worst impulses, or what Desmond Tutu (1931–2021) called our 'extraordinary capacity for evil'.

The sixth last word *completes* Christ's calling for us to be *conformed to the image of God*. The Scriptures declare that humankind is made in the 'image and likeness of God' (Genesis 1.26). Christians link being made in the image and likeness of God to Christ, 'the image of the invisible God' (Colossians 1.15). The passion narrative of John's Gospel points us towards what this image of God seen in Christ looks like. It manifests what it means to be conformed to that image. It shows us what it means to be fully human.

To see this, we can return to the beginning of John's passion narrative. Just before Jesus's arrest, trial and execution, John's Gospel records that 'Jesus knew that his hour had come.' At this moment, Jesus washes his disciples' feet and asks that they do likewise (John 13.1–20). It is an act of humble service. 'Just as I have loved you,' Jesus then commands, 'you also should love one another' (John 13.34). The washing of feet and command to love foreshadows how, 'having loved his own who were in the world, [Jesus] loved them to the end'. The cross perfects the *sight of love* to which we are commanded to conform. The cross manifests just how far Christ's love is willing to go. The cross shows what it means to love, and the power of that love. The cross allows us to see what it means for us to 'conform' to the image of Christ. The cross unveils *who we might become* – a human being shaped by love.

The sixth last word unveils, then, that true human fulfilment comes from self-emptying, not self-aggrandisement that pursues power, privilege and prestige. The latter disposition atrophies human connection and tends inexorably towards exclusion, conflict and violence. In contrast, self-emptying builds up the fullness of life together with God. As Pope Benedict puts it, in this sixth last word, we see that Jesus 'has accomplished the utter fullness of love – he has given himself'. Like Christ, we can align ourselves with the 'scum of the earth' (1 Corinthians 4.13) to interrupt and disrupt how the world works.

St Paul exhorts believers to 'let the same mind be in you that was in Christ Jesus' (Philippians 2.5–11). In an extended, hymn-like passage, St Paul explains that Jesus 'was in the form of God but emptied himself, taking the form of a servant'. 'Being found in human form,' St Paul continues, Jesus 'humbled himself and became obedient to the point of death – even death on a cross.' In this sixth last word, we see Jesus complete the sight of who we might be, should we imitate him in self-emptying. If we conform to the image of the crucified Christ – rather than the world that crucifies – we can be transformed by love (Romans 8.29, 12.2). We can be *little Christs* who point past what seems weak, foolish and scandalous. We can point towards the 'power of God' to make all things new. We can be perfected by the love we receive and become in the crucified Christ.

The sixth last word demands that we never forget that the cross *defies* apparent failure. Fleming Rutledge writes that 'it is the cross, and the cross alone, that seals [Jesus's] mission and, in retrospect, illuminates and explains all that preceded it'. We might also say that the cross, and the cross alone, illuminates everything that comes after it too. The cross fulfils how we know God and know ourselves. The cross interrupts our assumptions and everyday practices, even until this very day. It disrupts our ordinary ways of knowing and doing. The cross manifests a radical new understanding and a new way of being that defies the status quo as the final word. As the contemporary evangelist Rob Bell puts it, the sixth last word speaks that 'love wins'.

The cross gives a vision of how human history – past, present and future – converges and finds its true purpose in love. 'Having been made perfect,' the Epistle to the Hebrews writes, Jesus 'became the source of eternal salvation' (Hebrews 5.9). The Greek word for 'perfect' ('teleioun') used here has the same root as the word 'finished' ('tetelestai') – namely 'telos', meaning 'end', 'goal' or 'final purpose'. The cross is the *end of history*, meaning its perfection. The cross perfectly expresses God's love for us. Jesus fulfils God's loving will to free, cleanse, heal and renew those who are oppressed. On the cross, Jesus performs what Pope Benedict calls a 'cosmic liturgy'. The 'cosmic liturgy' of the cross is a perfect work that completes salvation for all times and places (Hebrews 10.10).

The sixth last word is freighted with prophetic significance in John's Gospel as a result. Jesus drinks the 'sour wine' prophesied in Psalm 69 as the drink of the rejected messiah. The branch of hyssop on which he is offered the sour wine recalls both the first Passover, where God freed the Israelites from Egyptian slavery (Exodus 12.22), and the ceremonial use of hyssop for purification (Psalm 51.7). Jesus now finally drinks 'the cup that the Father has given me' (John 18.11). Jesus on the cross confronts the entire human experience of physical and spiritual oppression. He disrupts it. We see in his self-emptying and sacrificial love that God defies it and speaks a new way and a new humanity.

This sixth last word declares that the 'power of God' – love itself – unfolds in our midst like a flower at dawn with unstoppable finality. The sixth last word is 'pregnant with our complete conversion', as Karl Barth evocatively described the Good News of Christ. It expresses the goal, end or purpose of God's love for us as a reality in our midst. One commentary accordingly calls the sixth last word a 'cry of triumph'. Even as Jesus dies, we see and know that *God is love and God is with us* (Matthew 1.23; compare Isaiah 7.4). Love lingers on the lips of the dying Christ – and is ready for resurrection.

There is still something *uncomfortable*, however, about this sixth last word. This discomfort should stop us from simply ending here in triumph. We must wrestle further with the *failure* with which we are still left – and learn to be chastened by the *failure of religious speech,* which is to say the failure of theology.

It is finished. In moral terms, humanity fails on the cross. We see how religion and politics combine in toxic fashion.

As such, religious speech itself fails on the cross. We see in brutal and inescapable focus the evil of which we are capable. We are confronted with how we continue to be complicit with the human tendency towards destructive evil in our own age. Religious speech or Christian faith does not save us from such proclivities. On the cross, we perceive how religious belief of any sort – no matter how noble or ancient – can degrade individuals and destroy communities. As history abundantly shows, religious certainty gains lethal force as it pursues prestige, power and privilege. Christianity is no exception to that terrible rule.

It is finished. The contemporary English theologian Marika Rose writes that, 'whichever way you look at it, theology has failed'. Whether Christianity remains intellectually or morally credible is an open question. The great doubters of religion – some of whom we have engaged with in this book – are right to be suspicious of Christianity. They are justified in decrying along with Arthur Schopenhauer (1788–1860) the 'horrors and absurdities of religion'. They have solid grounds to agree with him that 'in the eyes of a friend of truth every fraud, however pious, is still a fraud'.

Christians must learn to be chastened by failure. As Jesus's sixth last word fades, the words of Christians have proved too ready to fill the silence. For all its pious sound, the religious talk of Christian communities has led to countless little crucifixions. These little crucifixions flare like a conflagration beyond the sight of the cross. History now resurrects the voices of those whom Christianity (and white Christianity in particular) has crucified over the ages. As Marika Rose comments, 'the voices of those whom [Christianity] has oppressed [now] rise up to challenge its dominance and stand in judgement upon it'. For all its talk of love, Christianity more often has shown itself marked by *fear*. Christianity is now typically associated with racism, classism, misogyny, homophobia and transphobia. Christians are often popularly viewed with incredulity, suspicion and even contempt as a result. Christianity must, as Rose commends, 'confront…its own failure'.

Christian communities desperately need, then, what Rose calls a 'theology of failure'. Parts of the Christian tradition recognize, of course, that religious speech *fails*. These parts of the Christian tradition developed a 'theology of failure' as a result. We can turn to this tradition to help us confront the moral failings of religious communities and learn how to fail better.

Perhaps the greatest exponent of a 'theology of failure' was an unknown writer referred to as Pseudo-Dionysius or known more simply as Dionysius. He was a Syrian Christian thinker who wrote in the late fifth or early sixth century. The surviving writings of Pseudo-Dionysius include four treatises and ten letters. Two of his most influential works were the *Divine Names* and the *Mystical Theology*. In these works, Dionysius showed the possibilities and limits of religious speech as part of the Christian journey towards union with God. We will attend to *Divine Names* here because it is in this work that Dionysius considers how we can name God, and why this naming always fails. Dionysius developed two basic strategies for how we can talk about God. We can consider each strategy in turn. They unpack how Dionysius's 'theology of failure' sees the failure of religious speech as an integral and chastening feature of learning to fail upwards towards God.

The first strategy that Dionysius developed is known as 'kataphasis', a Greek word that means 'affirming'. It revolves around the sense in which we can positively declare certain things about who God is because of God's self-disclosure to us. For Dionysius, we depend upon revelation to know anything about God because God transcends creation. 'How can we speak of the divine names,' wonders Dionysius, 'if the Transcendent surpasses all discourse and all knowledge?' The way Dionysius recognizes God's transcendence is, of course, thoroughly biblical. 'My thoughts are not your thoughts,' says God, 'nor are your ways my ways' (Isaiah 55.8). It is God alone 'who has immortality and dwells in unapproachable light, whom no one has ever seen or can see' (1 Timothy 6.16). Yet, the Scriptures record God's self-disclosure in salvation history, perfected in Christ. The Scriptures allow us to 'name' an ineffably transcendent God. The scriptural names given to God show how God accommodates the 'immeasurable and infinite' character of God to the limits of human languages and capacities. God's self-disclosure allows us to name the unknowable God in some positive way.

In the Scriptures, Dionysius wrote, 'numerous symbols are employed to convey the varied attributes of what is imageless'. To populate what he means, Dionysius lists some of the biblical names given to God. The list includes names such as 'being', 'life', 'light', 'truth', 'good', 'beautiful', 'wise', 'beloved', 'mind', 'ancient of days' and 'King of kings'. Among many others, these names represent a positive way of affirmation (the so-called 'via positiva') by which we can speak something about God and know who God is.

The second strategy that Dionysius developed is known as 'apophasis', coming from a Greek word that means 'denial'. It revolves around the sense that even as we name God, we cannot forget that God transcends anything we might say about God. We must strip away what we think we know when we say anything about God. We must learn to deny or negate what we say about God because what we say will always fail to capture God adequately. We must shake our naming. We must not measure 'the divine by our human standards' but be willing to strip away what we think we understand or know to approach the God who 'transcends the nature of the mind'. All religious speech fails. We must also travel a negative way of denial, known as the 'via negativa'.

Let's take as an example of the strategy of denial the claim that 'God exists'. Now, Christians certainly talk about God as existing. Yet, God does not exist as, say, we exist. We exist in a contingent and limited fashion. We are born, we live as an embodied creature, and then we die. We only exist insofar as God creates, sustains and redeems us. By contrast, God exists perfectly, eternally and without limit, change or dependency upon anything. That might sound completely intelligible to us. But it doesn't mean we therefore fully understand what God's existence is really like. God is 'supra-existent being', as Dionysius puts it. God transcends our understanding and naming. We cannot fully understand what it means for God to exist. There is nothing like God in creation. Our language breaks down trying to capture who God is. There always remains what Karl Barth calls an 'infinite qualitative distinction' between God and creation. By this, Barth means Christianity proclaims a 'God utterly distinct from men' who is 'unapproachably distant and unutterably strange'. That radical distinction between God and creation means our language will always fail to capture who God is. We must acknowledge that failure of religious speech by negating, denying or stripping away what we think we know. We have to say that 'God does not exist' – not to deny God as real, but to remind ourselves that we can't fully grasp what that claim means.

As Dionysius developed these two strategies, his work narrated the sense in which people need to learn how to affirm and deny what they say about God in a circular fashion. God makes 'God' known. God makes 'God' speakable. But God still transcends us. God transcends the ability of our language to capture adequately who God is. We must strip away our language. We must deny what we think we know. The religious speaker must alternate between speaking and stripping away.

For Dionysius, then, the circular process of affirming and denying what we say about God was fundamentally a spiritual exercise. This spiritual exercise grounds us in God's self-disclosure. It clears away our concepts so that we always make room for God to speak. The circular process of affirming and denying purifies us. It allows us both to speak about God and avoid falling into idolatry.

Idolatry has always proved a difficult temptation to resist. As the French philosopher Simone Weil (1909–1943) once caustically remarked, 'the majority of the pious are idolaters'. She meant that when religious speech is not purified by self-awareness of its failure, it erects an idol to worship. It inevitably then offers human sacrifices to that idol. For this reason, Weil condemned, for example, Christian missionary efforts that followed on from colonial conquest. 'It was... never said by Christ,' Weil wrote, 'that those who bring the Gospel should be accompanied, even at a distance, by battleships.' Far from simply bringing Christ to Africa or Asia, Christian missionaries 'brought these territories under the cold, cruel, and destructive domination of the white race'. The complicity of Christianity with colonial conquest and its attendant racism witnessed to the moral failure of its religious speech.

By contrast, Dionysius's circular method of affirming and denying helps us avoid the temptation to domesticate God to our limited understanding. Dionysius teaches us that we will always fail to comprehend God. To 'comprehend' means to 'seize' something completely. If we think we comprehend God, then we claim we know all there is to know. We will always morally fail if we think we have mastered who God is. We fall prey to intractable dogmatism. From dogmatism flows the worst human instincts to force the world to conform with what we speak. We become ready to crucify others to protect the distortions of our religious speech, such as we find in the heresy of racism and white supremacy. We close ourselves off from being interrupted and disrupted by what the Scottish Jesuit Gerald Hughes (1924–2014) called the 'God of surprises'.

Dionysius's 'theology of failure' carries moral significance. It warns us of the peril of what happens when we think we can master who God is. In our contemporary age, for example, we see how Christianity has been historically complicit with ecological devastation, as well as the racist oppression of colonialism decried by Simone Weil. As the contemporary Black theologian Willie Jennings puts it, the spectre of the 'white self-sufficient man' defined by 'possession, mastery and control' haunts much religious speech. White, male, western Christianity saw itself as the pinnacle of religious understanding. It saw itself as having mastered who God is. It then sought to 'civilize' nature and the world through conquest and assimilation. It warped the scriptural mandate that humankind should exercise 'dominion' over creation to legitimate the exploitation and degradation of nature by western industry and capitalism (Genesis 1.26). It legitimated colonial expansion and entire systems of racism that continue to shape our society. When white people thought they had mastered religious speech, they turned into oppressive masters. They turned other people, or even the earth itself, into that which they oppressed – and all in the name of God.

The 'theology of failure' we see in Dionysius rejects that we possess, master and control God in any sense. In doing so, it awakens a chastened moral sensibility. His 'theology of failure' confronts the complicity of unchecked religious talk with oppression. Dionysius reminds us that we must always remain open to how God interrupts and disrupts our religious talk. The black feminist poet and critic Audre Lorde once said, 'the master's tools will never dismantle the master's house'. Dionysius's spiritual exercise of affirming and denying rejects that we can ever 'master' God or use our religious speech to position ourselves as 'masters' who can legitimately oppress others in the name of God. It chastens what we say and do. It prevents us erecting an idol of our imagination. It stops the human sacrifices we otherwise prove all too willing to make to such idols. It smashes these idols as the 'work of human hands' and a 'snare' that kills God's disruptive truth (Psalm 106.36). It offers hope in our own age that chastened religious talk can liberate us all as God interrupts and disrupts us.

It is finished. As we return to this sixth last word with a 'theology of failure', we can let it speak afresh to us about the failure of religious speech. In the sixth last word, we hear and see how Jesus perfects his saving work on the cross. This saving work interrupts and disrupts all claims to religious and political knowledge with a divine vision of a new way of being. Jesus on the cross sets what Karl Barth calls a 'question mark against all claims to truth'. After the cross, however, we cannot transpose this divine certainty into the conceited key that we now understand or possess God fully. Rather, the sixth last word and Dionysius remind us that we only ever *apprehend* God. The word 'apprehend' means 'to get hold of' or 'grasp'. We apprehend God because through the cross we have a handle-hold on that which is most true, namely God. We know *enough* to trust in the love we see – and be challenged by it.

In rock climbing, when people get a handle-hold, they know they are safe to begin to scale upwards. Yet, they continue to move tentatively, feeling their way, open to failure and falling. They move back and forth, aware that every move remains provisional, honest about frailty and risk but hopeful that they will eventually ascend. The rock climber is not a bad image for the Christian life and a 'theology of failure'.

It is finished. As the sixth last word fades to silence, it makes us confront the failure of religious speech. It suggests that we need to become theological atheists of a sort. We might think the use of the word 'atheist' a little facetious here. After all, the word 'atheist' derives from a Greek word that literally means 'without god'. But saying we need to become 'theological atheists' of a sort doesn't mean that we must begin denying the reality of God. Rather, it means that Christians must go even *further* than atheists tend to go. People of faith must learn to strip away the certainty of *everything* that they say about God. They must entertain the ways in which human speech, language and talk about God is frail, limited, inadequate, provisional and dangerous unless it's matched by humility, self-awareness and openness to the God of surprises.

The best last word on this sixth last word belongs to Denys Turner. Turner writes that 'in order to deny every kind of idolatry possible, a Christian *must be every kind of atheist possible*'. In becoming every kind of atheist possible, Christians can learn to deny that what they say about God has the last word on who God is or what God does. We might learn from Dionysius's 'theology of failure', should we return more often to it. We might fail better. We might fail upwards to God. By embracing a 'theology of failure' and the failure of our religious speech, we make room for God. We try our best to let God speak to us in Christ, whether from the cross of Good Friday or bursting from the empty tomb of Easter Sunday. We strive to hear like St Paul that it 'is no longer I who live, but it is Christ who lives in me' (Galatians 2.20).

'COMMEND'

It was now about noon, and darkness came over the whole land until three in the afternoon, while the sun's light failed; and the curtain of the temple was torn in two. Then Jesus, crying with a loud voice, said, 'Father, into your hands I commend my spirit.' Having said this, he breathed his last.

Luke 23.44–6

By an undivided and absolute abandonment of yourself and everything, shedding all and freed from all, you will be uplifted to the ray of the divine shadow which is above everything else.

Pseudo-Dionysius (late fifth to early sixth century)

The mystery of God is revealed in Christ and the Spirit as the mystery of love.

Catherine LaCugna (1952–1997)

Three hours after the falling of dusk over the cross, it all ends with a last word that speaks of *reunion*. In this seventh last word, Jesus addresses the Father who sent him into the world. Now, with his last breath, Jesus returns himself to this Father. As he dies, Jesus quotes the fifth verse of Psalm 31: 'into your hands, I commend my spirit'. In quoting from this psalm, Jesus invokes its entirety. This psalm prays for rescue. It also praises God for redemption. As such, the whole psalm expresses the drama of salvation we have witnessed unfolding on the cross. 'I am the scorn of all my adversaries,' the psalmist bewails, 'a horror to my neighbours.' 'Be gracious to me, O Lord, for I am in distress,' the psalmist pleads, 'my eye wastes away from grief, my soul and body also.' In this drama, the psalmist unconditionally gives himself over to God. 'Into your hand I commit my spirit,' the psalmist declares, 'you have redeemed me, O Lord, faithful God.' The three hours of the cross at the falling of dusk recapitulates this whole psalm. Just as the psalmist trusts in God, now in the darkest moment of lethal adversity, the Son entrusts his Spirit to the Father – and God speaks faithful redemption.

In this seventh last word of reunion, we listen into an intimate conversation that takes place in the trinitarian life of God. As he expires, Jesus breathes out the sound of the Holy Trinity. We hear the bond of overflowing love that unites God the Father, God the Son and God the Holy Spirit. This reading of the seventh last word as a trinitarian one may seem like a stretch, or less than obvious. But others have seen the Trinity revealed through the cross. The medieval theologian Julian of Norwich reflected at length upon her mystical visions of the crucified Christ. When 'Jesus appears', she wrote, 'the blessed Trinity is understood, as I *see* it.' As Julian pondered what the crucified Jesus was trying to show her in these mystical visions, she realized that 'love was his meaning'. For

Julian, the shape of this crucified love was trinitarian. 'The Trinity is our maker,' she perceived as she saw the crown of thorns piercing the flesh of Jesus on the cross. 'The Trinity is our protector,' she continued, 'the Trinity is our everlasting lover, the Trinity is our endless joy and our bliss.' All this love she saw through the diaphanous pain of the cross.

In this seventh last word, we too see that 'love was his meaning'. Like Julian of Norwich, we hear how the sound of this crucified love is trinitarian. On the cross, we see Jesus fulfil the will of the Father who has sent his Son for us, out of love (John 5.36). In this seventh last word, we hear in Luke's Gospel Jesus 'commend' his 'spirit' back to the Father before he 'breathed his last'. John's Gospel puts it slightly differently: Jesus 'gave up his spirit' as he dies. This all may sound like Luke and John employ euphemisms to say that 'Jesus died'. An even older English translation of these passages compounds this sense when it translates the original Greek as saying that Jesus 'gave up the ghost'. The original Greek in Luke and John's Gospel, however, suggests something potentially far richer about this moment and last word. The Greek word in both these passages for 'spirit' is 'pneuma'. This Greek word means 'breath'. It carries a sense of something like 'the animating force of who someone is'. But the same word is most used in the New Testament to describe the Holy Spirit. We can understand that Jesus refers, then, to the Holy Spirit, and not simply to himself. Luke uses the verb 'paratithemai' to suggest that Jesus 'commits', 'commends' or 'entrusts' this Spirit. John uses the verb 'paredoken' to intimate that Jesus 'hands over', 'gave' or 'delivered' the Spirit. We might better render, then, these passages about the death of Jesus as saying that he 'handed over' or 'entrusted his Spirit' – meaning the Holy Spirit.

In the seventh last word Jesus hands over or entrusts the Holy Spirit who breathes the power of God's life and love. Jesus exhales this Spirit as he expires. This Spirit has animated who Jesus is and what he does. The Holy Spirit 'overshadowed' Mary with God's power when she conceived Jesus (Luke 1.35). The Spirit made our human nature a 'new creation' through the incarnation, just as the 'spirit of God' brooded over the depths in the first creation story (Genesis 1.2). The Holy Spirit descended upon Jesus at his baptism and the Father declared him beloved (Luke 3.22). The same Spirit remained with Jesus, filling him with power (Luke 4.1–2, 14). Now, in the final breath of the cross, Jesus breathes this Holy Spirit, the breath of God, back to the Father. In this seventh last word we see, in a sense, the reunion of the Holy Trinity. It unveils the intimate life of love in which the Father, Son and Spirit mutually indwell one another. It reveals how Father, Son and Spirit always work together in love, out of love for that which they have created, to bring that creation back to love.

Jesus may address this seventh last word of loving reunion to the Father, but we hear and are spoken into it too. 'Everything written here is a mirror for us,' Augustine of Hippo (354–430) would write of the psalms. Augustine thinks 'we discover our voice' in the psalms as one with the voice of Christ. As Jesus speaks the words of Psalm 31.5, they are ours also: 'Father, into your hands I commend my spirit.' The intimate reunion scene of the seventh last word is pregnant with the promise that we can return to and be reunited with God.

Those who follow Jesus became caught up in his trinitarian life and love. We see this dynamic described in the Scriptures. After the resurrection, Jesus breathes the Holy Spirit over those who follow him (John 20.22). The Holy Spirit – the animating breath of God that Jesus breathes out and returns to the Father – now 'indwells' believers (Romans 8.9) and 'adopts' them into the inner life of God (Romans 8.15). The Spirit enfolds people into love itself. Through the divine breath breathed by the Son sent by the Father, we become one with God. 'United with God, we live, as it were, the life of God,' as the Elizabethan divine Richard Hooker (1554–1600) put it. In this seventh last word, we hear the whisper of how we might be captured, caught up and reunited with the loving heart of the Trinity who has made, sustained and redeemed us. We hear what Julian of Norwich saw in her mystical visions of the crucified Christ.

At the falling of dusk, at a moment of what seems like supreme failure, the seventh last word speaks of how the Trinity stands for and with us in our utter brokenness. Union with the Trinity is the final word about who God is and who we are called to be. Jesus perfects our sight of this loving Trinity on the cross. This seventh last word refuses the cross the last word. It defeats horror by speaking eternal, divine *love* as the final and perfect speech that disrupts all that opposes love. With his dying breath, Jesus breathes out the trinitarian life of God into our lungs.

Having said this, he breathed his last. After speaking this seventh last word, Jesus nevertheless *ends* here – he dies. The breath that gave him speech now expires. The seventh last word turns over to silence. His religious talk *fails* at this moment.

The seventh last word is one of *surrender* as much as it is of reunion. Jesus surrenders to God beyond speech. We cannot jump straight to Easter and the glory of the resurrection from here. We can ignore neither the mauled muteness at the end of the cross, nor the stony silence of the taciturn tomb. We must confront the failure of religious speech and discern what to make of it in relation to the Christian life. The heart of the cross is the Trinity. Or, rather, the cross takes us into the heart of the Trinity – a mystery that can never be truly comprehended or mastered, but which fully comprehends us. We must enter the silence that ends this seventh last word.

This seventh last word asks us to return, then, to the 'theology of failure' and extend the kind of 'theological atheism' we explored in our last meditation. It asks us to return to that unknown theologian who wrote in the late fifth and early sixth centuries simply known as 'Dionysius'. It asks us to consider how Dionysius explores what union with the Trinity means in another of his major works called *Mystical Theology*.

Mystical Theology is a short work that follows on from *Divine Names* that we explored in the previous meditation on the sixth last word. Dionysius opens *Mystical Theology* with an invocatory prayer to the Trinity. He prays for God to 'lead us up beyond unknowing and light' to 'where the mysteries of God's Word lie simple, absolute and unchangeable in the brilliant darkness of a hidden silence'. Dionysius prays that 'the wholly unsensed and unseen' will 'completely fill our sightless minds'. The goal of the Christian life is union with God. The spiritual life for Dionysius ultimately involves, then, leaving behind 'everything perceived and understood' and 'unknowing' everything we think we know. As such, for Dionysius, union with God is a 'divine darkness', a startling image that suggests how God is 'beyond all being and knowledge'. Union with God requires total surrender and the 'inactivity of all knowledge'.

In *Mystical Theology*, then, Dionysius intensifies his 'theology of failure' developed in *Divine Names*. We saw in that last meditation how Dionysius developed in *Divine Names* a spiritual exercise of affirming and negating what we know about God. These are often called the 'via positiva' and 'via negativa', meaning the 'positive way' and 'negative way' respectively of naming God and yet denying that we fully comprehend who God is. Held together, these two ways as a spiritual exercise aimed to chasten our theological talk, remind us of God's transcendence beyond our comprehension, and help us avoid idolatry. This spiritual exercise represents a kind of 'theological atheism' that purifies our religious talk and inhibits our tendency to offer human sacrifice to the idols of our imaginations.

Ultimately, however, in *Mystical Theology*, Dionysius sees that the religious person must be ready to be *silent*. After all, the transcendent God stands beyond all affirmation and negation. The religious person must open themselves up, know the limits of their language, purify their understanding and at the end *surrender* to God's self-disclosure. This waiting silence is known as the 'way of eminence' or 'via eminentia'. We depend upon God's self-disclosure to be able to say anything about God. While God 'alone dwells in inaccessible light', God reveals who God is through the history of salvation recorded in the Scriptures. Likewise, we depend upon God to bring us to union with God. It would seem impossible for us as finite, limited, frail creatures to be able to enjoy union with an utterly transcendent God. Yet, such union with God is what God promises. We live in the waiting silence of this promise. As St Paul puts it, 'for now we see in a mirror, dimly, but then we will see face to face. Now I know only in part; then I will know fully, even as I have been fully known' (1 Corinthians 13.12). The waiting silence shows the radical priority of God's self-giving grace.

In *Mystical Theology*, then, Dionysius developed a further spiritual exercise to prepare believers for union with God, a union that interrupts and disrupts us completely. God is beyond naming and un-naming. God is beyond the 'via positiva' and 'via negativa'. God is beyond our positive statements of who God is. God is beyond even the negative stripping away of those statements. God is 'beyond assertion and denial'. God 'cannot be spoken of' and 'cannot be grasped by understanding'. To know God – and to be united with God – we must surrender to God. We must deny everything we think we know – and all so that God alone speaks into our silence, until we see God face-to-face.

Dionysius reminds us that whatever we say about God, ultimately 'our safest eloquence is silence', as the Elizabethan theologian Richard Hooker put it, 'for his glory is inexplicable, his greatness above our capacity and reach'. Dionysius says that after the circular act of affirming and denying, there follows a divine silence. While that silence may sound ominous, for Dionysius it is the hinterland of how God interrupts, disrupts and illumines us. Dionysius uses Moses as a biblical example of what he means by all of this. Just as Moses ascends into the darkness of Mount Sinai's peak to meet with God (Exodus 19.20), so too we rise through the 'mysterious darkness of unknowing' to God. Then God speaks to us of who God is and who we are in God, all without the mediation of human words. 'By an unaided and absolute abandonment of yourself and everything,' Dionysius wrote, 'shedding all and freed from all, you will be uplifted to the ray of the divine shadow which is above everything that is.' In darkness, we are reunited with God and united with the Trinity. This reunion is beyond human imagining and language, all of which we must abandon and surrender. At the end, all religious speech fails, and all our understanding about God is stripped away. We meet God after being purged by a 'theology of failure'. We meet God after a lifelong spiritual exercise that renders us, in a sense, as 'theological atheists' who deny we comprehend anything about God at all.

We perhaps might find all this talk of a 'theology of failure', 'theological atheism' and union with the Holy Trinity as rather abstract, strange and remote from our everyday concerns. It is, however, thoroughly practical. The Jewish scholar and historian Amos Funkenstein (1937–1995) famously claimed 'how much more deadly to theology were its helpers than its enemies'. Religious communities too often fail to attend to the frailty and limits of their religious talk. As a result, all too often religious communities morally fail too. To be morally or intellectually credible, religious communities must embrace the failure of their religious talk. They must open themselves up to the interruption and disruption of God. At the end, religious communities must attend to silence so they can listen for God to speak.

As we return to this seventh last word as a word of reunion and surrender, it turns us to the nature of God as a Trinity bonded by love. Such trinitarian love interrupts and disrupts us, capturing us into the inner life of God. The divine life is our life too. As the feminist Catholic theologian Catherine LaCugna (1952–1997) wrote, 'the doctrine of the Trinity is ultimately a practical doctrine with radical consequences for Christian life'. For LaCugna, 'the mystery of God is revealed in Christ and the Spirit as the mystery of love, the mystery of persons in communion who embrace death, sin and all forms of alienation for the sake of life'. The keyword here is 'mystery'. This doesn't mean something like 'an unsolved riddle' in the manner of, say, a murder mystery. Rather the theological idea of 'mystery' embraces the sense in which we cannot comprehend God and God's doings, but we can lean into them and be transformed by them as God self-discloses. In the cross – and in this seventh last word – we hear the 'mystery' of the Trinity and love spoken. We see this trinitarian life of love inviting us in. Jesus reveals who God is and what it means to be fully human. The Spirit he entrusts back to the Father in this seventh last word is the same Spirit who enfolds us into the Body of Christ. The Spirit he breathes he also breathes into us so that 'we become by grace what God is by nature', as Athanasius of Alexandria (296–373) put it. For LaCugna, this means that Jesus speaks how we might be 'persons in full communion with God and with every creature'.

The seventh last word commends we lean into the failure of our theological speech as an integral precondition for union with God. The falling of dusk and silence on the cross is pregnant with possibility. Darkness and silence chasten, purify and open us up to the Trinity as it speaks love. Surrendering to the 'darkness of unknowing' opens us up to all the ways in which that divine life of love interrupts and disrupts the ways in which we act destructively because of what we think we know. As we listen, we learn to attend to the silence of the tomb where Jesus is buried. In silence, we await resurrection and new life saturated by love.

At the close, then, this seventh last word – and indeed, each of the seven last words – speaks of how doubt is not the enemy of faith. Rather, doubt serves faith. Doubt commends, turns, entrusts, hands us over to the silence of the cross where God truly speaks without mediation. The falling of dusk on the cross is the fertile beginning of what it means to be united with God and see the world transformed through that union. At the end, the final, mysterious word on God and on us is simply this – *love*.

EPILOGUE: 'TRULY'

Now when the centurion, who stood facing him, saw that in this way he breathed his last, he said, 'Truly this man was God's Son!'

Mark 15.39

Now when the centurion and those with him, who were keeping watch over Jesus, saw the earthquake and what took place, they were terrified and said, 'Truly this man was God's Son!'

Matthew 27.54

When the centurion saw what had taken place, he praised God and said, 'Certainly this man was innocent.'

Luke 23.47

But the cross does not end in silence. It provokes an immediate response. The seven last words of Christ are not the only words to be spoken around the cross. The Gospels of Mark, Matthew and Luke all record the words of the Roman centurion as Jesus breathes his last. Luke's centurion declares that Jesus was 'innocent', and 'all the crowds who had gathered there for this spectacle... returned home, beating their breasts'. Mark and Matthew's centurion more pointedly declares that 'truly, this man was God's Son'. Whatever the words spoken, the centurion shows himself interrupted, disrupted and surprised by this crucified man who shows something of the life of God. The centurion's words, in whatever form they took, were his response to the perennial question asked by Jesus – 'who do you say that I am?' (Mark 8.29; Matthew 16.15; Luke 9.20).

We don't end in silence, either, even if we are called to rest in it. The seven last words carry beyond the falling of dusk on the cross. They speak to us as twilight settles on our certainties, shaking what we know and do. They speak into the crosses we bear or make others carry. We are called to respond to the seven last words. We are called to read ourselves into them. We are called to answer, through all our certain faith and uncertain doubts, who we say Jesus truly is – and who we truly might be as a result.

At the falling of dusk, the best last word is ours. Our last word will undoubtedly fail – but it might fail upwards into the new life of resurrection. This is our hopeful journey into darkness.

NOTES

All biblical references are taken from *The Holy Bible. New Revised Standard Version* (New York: OUP, 1996) unless otherwise stated.

INTRODUCTION: THE FALLING OF DUSK

'what is to be despised…what is to be hoped for in eternity', Augustine of Hippo, Epistle 140.5, in *The Works of St Augustine. Letters 100–155*, II/2, translated by Roland Teske (Hyde City: New City Press, 2002), p. 251.

'the cross alone is our theology', Martin Luther, *Commentary on the Psalms,* in *D. Martin Luthers Werke: Kritische Gesamtausgabe* (Weimar: Hermann Böhlaus Nachfolger, 1883–), vol. 5, p. 176.

'a very human response to think oneself abandoned', Ambrose of Milan, *On the Christian Faith*, 2.7.56, in *Nicene and Post-Nicene Fathers*, Second Series, vol. 10, edited by Philip Schaff and Henry Wace (Peabody: Hendrickson, 2004), p. 230.

'those who believe too much and those who believe too little', Terry Eagleton, *Culture and the Death of God* (New Haven: Yale University Press, 2014), p. 198.

'there is in God…/A deep but dazzling darkness', Henry Vaughan, 'The Night', in *Henry Vaughan: The Complete Poems* (Penguin, 1976), and widely anthologized.

'become what we are…bring us to be even what He is Himself', Irenaeus, *Against Heresies* 5, in *The Ante-Nicene Fathers,* vol. 1, edited by Alexander Roberts and James Donaldson (Peabody: Hendrickson, 2004), p. 526.

'only an atheist can be a good Christian…', Ernst Bloch, *Atheism in Christianity: the Religion of the Exodus and the Kingdom*, translated by J.T. Swann (New York: Herder & Herder, 1972), p.9.

CHAPTER ONE: 'FORGIVE'

'the person who asks forgiveness…the safety of being locked into the position of the offended victim', Rowan Williams, *Being Disciples. Essentials of the Christian Life* (London: SPCK, 2016), p. 39.

'was a form of advertisement…this person is the scum of the earth…more an insect than a human being', Fleming Rutledge, *The Crucifixion. Understanding the Death of Jesus Christ* (Grand Rapids: Eerdmans, 2015), p. 92.

'the utterly vile death of the cross', Origen, *Commentary on Matthew*, 27.22, quoted in Martin Hengel, *Crucifixion in the Ancient World and the Folly of Message of the Cross* (Philadelphia: Fortress, 1977), p. xi.

'all the evil impulses of the human race came to focus in him', Rutledge, *The Crucifixion*, p. 97.

'God lets himself be pushed out of the world on to the cross', Dietrich Bonhoeffer, 'Letter to Eberhard Bethge, dated 16 July 1944', in *Dietrich Bonhoeffer. Letters and Papers from Prison*, translated by Reginald Fuller (London: SCM, 1971), pp. 359–61.

'I like your Christ…you Christians are so unlike your Christ', Mahatma Gandhi, apocryphal and of uncertain origin.

'**Jesus foretold the Kingdom, and it was the Church that came**', Alfred Loisy, *The Gospel and the Church*, trans. Christopher Home (New York: Charles Scribner's Sons, 1912), p. 166.

'**masters of suspicion**', a term coined by Paul Ricoeur, *Freud and Philosophy: An Essay in Interpretation*, translated by Denis Savage (New Haven: Yale University Press, 1970), passim.

'**there was really only one Christian, and he died on the cross**', Friedrich Nietzsche, *The Anti-Christ* 39, in *Nietzsche: The Anti-Christ, Ecce Homo, Twilight of the Idols, and Other Writings*, translated by Judith Norman (Cambridge: CUP, 2005), p. 65.

'**the Christians have never practiced the actions Jesus prescribed them**', Friedrich Nietzsche, *The Will to Power* 191, in *The Complete Works of Friedrich Nietzsche*, vol. 14, edited by Oscar Levy (Edinburgh: Foulis, 1914), p. 158.

'**God is dead**', Friedrich Nietzsche, *The Gay Science* 108, 125, in *Nietzsche: The Gay Science* translated by Josefine Nauckhoff (Cambridge: CUP, 2003), pp. 109, 120.

'**true or anthropological essence of religion**', Ludwig Feuerbach, *The Essence of Christianity*, translated by Marian Evans (Cambridge: CUP, 2011), Title to Part I.

'**suspicious explanations**', Andrew Cole, *Reframing the Masters of Suspicion. Marx, Nietzsche, and Freud* (London: Bloomsbury, 2019), p. 2.

'**good = noble = powerful = beautiful = happy = blessed**', Friedrich Nietzsche, *On the Genealogy of Morality* I.7, in *Nietzsche. On the Genealogy of Morality*, translated by Carol Diethe (Cambridge: CUP, 2010), p. 17.

'**unfathomable...hatred of the powerless...love grew out of hatred...dangerous bait**', Nietzsche, *On the*

Genealogy of Morality I.7–8, in *Nietzsche. On the Genealogy of Morality*, pp. 17–19.

'I condemn Christianity... the one immortal blot on humanity', Nietzsche, *The Anti-Christ* 62, in *Nietzsche: The Anti-Christ*, p. 65.

'a form of redemption that would work for a post-the-istic age', Giles Fraser, *Redeeming Nietzsche. On the Piety of Unbelief* (London: Routledge, 2002), p. 2.

'the non-violent resistance of evil... in my guts I still want to punch you back', Fraser, *Redeeming Nietzsche*, p. 147.

'the child of Christianity...wounding vengeance, not eliminating it...interiorization of weakened vengeance...survives the impact of Christianity', René Girard, 'Nietzsche Versus the Crucified', in *The Girard Reader*, edited by J.G. Williams (New York: Crossroad, 1996), p. 252.

'grace without discipleship...living and incarnate', Dietrich Bonhoeffer, *The Cost of Discipleship* (London: SCM, 2001), p.4.

'remorseful apology...past promised to us', Mpho Tutu van Furth, *Forgiveness and Reparation, The Healing Journey* (London: DLT, 2022), p. 18.

CHAPTER TWO: 'BE'

'not possible to separate the Garden from the Kingdom', Giorgio Agamben, *The Kingdom and the Garden*, translated by Adam Kotsko (London: Seagull Books, 2020), p.4.

'Adam was in paradise, and paradise was in him', St Innocent of Alaska, *Indication of the Way into the Kingdom of Heaven: An Introduction to Christian Life* (Holy Trinity Publications, 2013), chapter 1.

'the determinative event...economy of salvation', Agamben, *The Kingdom and the Garden*, p. 15.

'fragrant meadow of this present paradise', St Cyril of Jerusalem, *Mystagogical Catechesis*, in *St. Cyril of Jerusalem: Lectures on the Christian Sacraments*, edited by F. L. Cross (Crestwood: St Vladimir's Seminary Press, 1995), I.1.

'while you are living...gladly expects your arrival', Ephrem the Syrian, *De paradiso Eden*, 2[7].2, quoted in Agamben, *The Kingdom and the Garden*, p. 10.

'a sign of weakness, ugliness, failure, incomprehension', Rutledge, *The Crucifixion*, p. 19.

'religion is the opium of the people', Karl Marx, *Critique of Hegel's Philosophy of Right*, in *Marx on Religion*, edited by John Raines (Philadelphia: Temple University Press, 2002), p. 171.

'the point is to change it', Karl Marx, *Concerning Feuerbach*, in *Marx on Religion*, p. 184.

'the history...of class struggles', Karl Marx and Friedrich Engels, *The Communist Manifesto: A Modern Edition*, translated by Eric Hobsbawm (London: Verso, 1998), p. 34.

'the proletarians...have a world to win!', Marx and Engels, *The Communist Manifesto*, p. 95.

'man makes religion...world of man...spiritual aroma...religion is the halo...opium of the people', Marx, *Critique of Hegel's Philosophy of Right*, in *Marx on Religion*, p. 171.

'the more of himself man gives to God, the less he has left in himself', Karl Marx, *Estranged Labour*, in *Marx on Religion*, p. 119.

'the parson has ever gone hand in hand with the landlord', Marx and Engels, *The Communist Manifesto*, p. 64.

'dominant strategy... to neutralize [the] political implications', Agamben, *The Kingdom and the Garden*, p. 3.

'like the Hebrew prophets... passion for truth and justice...the exploited and marginalized', John Raines, *Marx on Religion* (Philadelphia: Temple University Press, 2002), pp. 4–5.

'neither a territorial realm...the power of God is enacted', Elizabeth Conde-Frazier, *Atando Cabos: Latinx Contributions to Theological Education* (Eerdmans, 2021), p. 38, quoting Padilla DeBorst.

'has not assumed he has not healed', Gregory of Nazianzus, Letter 101, in *Nicene and Post-Nicene Fathers*, Second Series, vol. 7, edited by Philip Schaff and Henry Wace (Peabody: Hendrickson, 2004), p. 440.

'the Gospel depicts...with the language and symbols of imperial rule', William Carter, *Matthew and Empire: Initial Explorations* (Trinity Press, 2001), pp. 89–90.

'the bullet...spiritual subjugation', Ngũgĩ wa Thiong'o, *Decolonizing the Mind: The Politics of Language in African Literature* (Oxford: James Currey/Heinemann, 1986, repr. 2005), p. 9.

'the concept...kin to each other...in which we can fully live', Ada María Isasi-Díaz, 'Defining Our "Proyecto Histórico": "Mujerista" Strategies for Liberation', *Journal of Feminist Studies in Religion*, vol. 9, nos. 1–2 (1993), pp. 17–28.

CHAPTER THREE: 'BEHOLD'

'the church...is a social ethic', Stanley Hauerwas, *The Peaceable Kingdom: A Primer in Christian Ethics* (Notre Dame: UNDP, 1983), p. 99.

'a repackaging...aggressively anti-religious rhetoric', Steven Kettell, 'What's really new about New Atheism?', *Palgrave Communications* 2 (2016), https://doi.org/10.1057/palcomms.2016.99.

'the life of the church is a series of always failing experiments', Mike Higton, *The Life of Christian Doctrine* (T&T Clark, 2020), p. 4.

'dare to know', Immanuel Kant, 'What is the Enlightenment?', in *Practical Philosophy*. Translated by Mary J. Gregor (Cambridge: Cambridge University Press, 1999), p. 17.

'universal acid...mindless, algorithmic process', Daniel Dennett, *Darwin's Dangerous Idea* (London: Penguin, 1995), p. 63.

'no future in a sacred myth', Dennett, *Darwin's Dangerous Idea*, p. 22.

'I for one...all the answers', Daniel Dennett, *Breaking the Spell: Religion as a Natural Phenomenon* (New York: Viking, 2007), p. 51.

'the designer hypothesis...who designed the designer?', Richard Dawkins, *The God Delusion* (London: Bantam Press, 2006), p. 188.

'theory of religion...a misfiring of something useful', Dawkins, *God Delusion*, p. 218.

'divisive force...a label for in-group/out-group enmity and vendetta', Dawkins, *God Delusion*, p. 294.

'in a world riven by ignorance...astonishing degree', Sam Harris, *An Atheist Manifesto* (7 December, 2007), https://www.samharris.org/blog/an%E2%80%93atheist%E2%80%93 manifesto.

'the only angels we need invoke... masterpiece', Sam Harris, *The End of Faith: Religion, Terror, and the Future of Reason* (New York: Norton, 2004), p. 226.

'exceptional claims of religion...dismissed without evidence', Christopher Hitchens, *God Is Not Great: Religion Poisons Everything* (New York: Hachette Twelve, 2007), pp. 150, 258.

'violent, irrational, intolerant...on its conscience', Hitchens, *God Is Not Great*, p. 56.

'religion...new enlightenment', Hitchens, *God Is Not Great*, p. 282.

'it is interesting to find...Nazis or Stalinists', Hitchens, *God Is Not Great*, p. 230.

'adoption arrangement', Pope Benedict, *Jesus of Nazareth. Part Two* (San Francisco: Ignatius Press, 2011), p. 220.

'a good caudle of broth to comfort her', *The Book of Margery Kempe*, translated by Anthony Bale (Oxford: Oxford University Press, 2015), p. 175.

'she will cherish thee...from her Son', *Great Commentary of Cornelius à Lapide*, translated by Thomas Mossman (Edinburgh: John Grant, 1908), vol. 6, John 19.27.

'received her into his inner life setting', Pope Benedict, *Jesus of Nazareth*, p. 221.

'a journey deeper...existing patterns of the church's life', Higton, *Life of Christian Doctrine*, p. 5.

'the cross represents...so too is that power', Kelly Brown Douglas, *Stand Your Ground: Black Bodies and the Justice of God* (Orbis, 2015), p. 182.

CHAPTER FOUR: 'WHY?'

'brings the irreligiousness of the cross into sharp focus', Rutledge, *Crucifixion*, p. 97.

'it is not his divinity that doubts, but his human soul', Ambrose of Milan, *On the Christian Faith*, 2.7.56, in *Nicene and Post-Nicene Fathers*, Second Series, vol. 10, edited by Philip Schaff and Henry Wace (Peabody: Hendrickson, 2004), p. 230.

'the voice of human weakness…speech of human infirmity', Epistle 140.5–6, in *The Works of St Augustine. Letters 100–155*, II/2, translated by Roland Teske (Hyde City: New City Press, 2002), pp. 251–2.

'this means…little while was concealed', John Calvin, *1538 Catechism of the Church of Geneva*, 20.4, in *Calvin's First Catechism: A Commentary* (Louisville: WJK, 1997), pp. 23–4; the final comment is taken from Calvin's *1545 Catechism*, p. 68.

'no persuasive argument…feeling forsaken expressed in the psalm quote', Raymond Brown, *Death of the Messiah. From Gethsemane to the Grave* (New Haven: Yale University Press, 1998), p. 1051.

'Epicurus's old questions are yet to be answered… whence then is evil?', David Hume, *Dialogues Concerning Natural Religion*, Book X (Hackett, 1998), p. 63.

'there is hardly anything more obvious…colossal reality', Martin Luther King, 'The Death of Evil Upon the Seashore', in *The Papers of Martin Luther King, Jr. Volume VI: Advocate of the Social Gospel* (University of California Press, 2007), p. 505.

'more religiously imperative…divinity as well?', Rowan Williams, *Wrestling with angels: conversations in modern theology*, edited by Mike Higton (London: SCM Press, 2007), pp. 272–3.

'detached from traditional patterns of Christian thinking about God', Karen Kilby, 'Evil and the Limits of Theology', *New Blackfriars*, vol. 84, no. 983 (2003), p. 14.

'necessarily incomprehensible and inexplicable to us as human beings', Karl Barth, *Church Dogmatics, III/3*, §50.3 (Edinburgh: T & T Clark, 1961), p. 311.

'the so-called…completely legitimate and as utterly unanswerable', Kilby, 'Evil and the Limits of Theology', p. 24.

'having once truly tasted…cleave to God', Richard Hooker, 'Certaintie', in *The Folger Library Edition of the Works of Richard Hooker*, edited by W. Speed Hill, vol. 5 (Cambridge: Belknap Press, 1990), pp. 69–71.

'Jesus Christ is not a quick answer…portrayed in crucifixion', Kosuke Koyama, *Mount Fuji and Mount Sinai: A Critique of Idols* (London: SCM Press, 1984), p. 241.

CHAPTER FIVE: 'THIRST'

'God thirsts to be thirsted for', Augustine of Hippo, *De diversis quaestionibus octoginta tribus*, 64.4, quoted in *Catechism of the Catholic Church*, para. 2560.

'in your thirst, Lord…save all of humanity', Pope Francis, Address on Good Friday, Palatine Hill, 3 April 2015, available on https://www.vatican.va.

'our hearts…until they rest in you', Augustine, *Confessions*, Book I, translated by Henry Chadwick (Oxford: OUP, 2008), p. 3.

'agitate the sleep of mankind', Sigmund Freud, quoted in P. Gay, *Freud: A Life for Our Time* (New York: Norton, 1988), p. xvii.

'the knowledge and skills…that satisfy human needs', Sigmund Freud, *The Future of an Illusion* (Penguin Great Ideas, 2008), pp. 2–3.

'mental assets', Freud, *Future of an Illusion*, pp. 10–13.

'the main function of culture…white Christian culture', Freud, *Future of an Illusion*, pp. 16, 20, 22.

'a neurotic who is cured…favourable conditions', Sigmund Freud, 'Transference', in *Standard Edition of the Complete Psychological Works of Sigmund Freud* (Vintage, 1999), vol. 16, p. 435.

'why are…what are they actually worth?', Freud, *Future of an Illusion*, p. 22.

'very remarkable…feeblest authentication of all', Freud, *Future of an Illusion*, p. 32.

'armed with this information…the secret of their strength is the strength of those desires', Freud, *Future of an Illusion*, pp. 36–8.

'scientific work…knowledge outside of ourselves', Freud, *Future of an Illusion*, pp. 38–9.

'lost cause…that which science cannot give us', Freud, *Future of an Illusion*, pp. 68, 72.

'have had the courage…from the animal world', William Morton Wheeler, quoted in Richard Webster, *Freud* (London: Weidenfeld and Nicolson, 2003), p. 5.

'the right place…in the minds that create (and continually recreate) it', H. Whitehouse, 'Why Do We Need Cognitive Theories of Religion?', in *Religion as a Human Capacity*, edited by T. Light & B.C. Wilson (Leiden: Brill, 2004), p. 71.

'ritual celebration…castration…quintessential…inferiority…non-offensive ornament', James Cone, *The Cross and the Lynching Tree* (Maryknoll: Orbis, 2011), pp. xiii–xiv, 7, 9, 94.

'help us see Jesus…light', Cone, *Cross and the Lynching Tree*, p. xix.

'God took the evil…into the triumphant beauty of the divine', Cone, *Cross and the Lynching Tree*, p. 166.

'a story about God's presence…close off any future', Cone, *Cross and the Lynching Tree*, pp. 26, 150.

'both the cross…determine our final meaning', Cone, *Cross and the Lynching Tree*, p. 3.

CHAPTER SIX: 'FINISHED'

'slaves, enemy soldiers…lowest regard in society', Brown Douglas, *Stand Your Ground*, p. 174.

'horror-defeater', Marilyn McCord Adams, *Christ and Horrors. The Coherence of Christology* (Cambridge: CUP, 2006), ch. 3.

'extraordinary capacity for evil', Desmond Tutu, quoted by Brown Douglas, *Stand Your Ground*, p. 180.

'has accomplished…he has given himself', Pope Benedict, *Jesus*, p. 223.

'it is the cross…all that preceded it', Rutledge, *Crucifixion*, p. 61.

'cosmic liturgy', Pope Benedict, *Jesus*, p. 223.

'whichever way you look at it, theology has failed', Marika Rose, *A Theology of Failure* (New York: Fordham, 2019), p. 1.

'in the eyes…is still a fraud', Arthur Schopenhauer, *The Horrors and Absurdities of Religion* (Penguin Great Ideas, 2009), p. 17.

'the voices…stand in judgement upon it…its own failure', Rose, *Theology of Failure*, p. 2.

'how can we speak…all knowledge', Dionysius, *Complete Works*, translated by Colm Luibheid (New York: Paulist Press, 1987), p. 53.

'numerous symbols…imageless', Dionysius, *Complete Works*, p. 52.

'infinite qualitative distinction', Karl Barth, *The Humanity of God* (Louisville: Westminster John Knox Press, 1960), p. 42.

'God utterly distinct from men…strange', Karl Barth, *Epistle to the Romans* (London: OUP, 1933), pp. 27–8.

'the majority of the pious are idolaters', Simone Weil, *First and Last Notebooks*, translated by Richard Rees (Eugene: Wipf and Stock, 2015), p. 308.

'it was…domination of the white race', Simone Weil, *Selected Essays*, translated by Richard Rees (London: OUP, 1962), p. 197, and *Letter to a Priest*, translated by A.F. Wills (London: Routledge, 2002), p. 18.

'white self-sufficient…and control', Willie Jennings, *After Whiteness: An Education in Belonging* (Grand Rapids: Eerdmans, 2020), p. 6.

'**the master's tools will never dismantle the master's house**', Audre Lorde, quoted in Brown Douglas, *Stand Your Ground*, p. 183.

'**question mark against all claims to truth**', Barth, *Epistle to the Romans*, p. 35.

'**in order…every kind of atheist possible**', Denys Turner, 'Apophaticism, idolatry and the claims of reason', in *Silence and the Word: Negative Theology and Incarnation*, edited by Oliver Davies and Denys Turner (Cambridge: CUP, 2002), p. 19.

CHAPTER SEVEN: 'COMMEND'

'**Jesus appears…love was his meaning…bliss**', Julian of Norwich, *Showings* (Paulist Press, 1978), pp. 175, 181.

'**everything…discover our voice**', Augustine of Hippo, *Enarrationes*, 30(2).3, in *Expositions of the Psalms* (Hyde Park: New City Press, 2000), vol. 1, pp. 322–4; and *Enarrationes*, 40.6; 45.1, in *Expositions of the Psalms*, vol. 2, pp. 231–2; 310–11.

'**united with God, we live, as it were, the life of God**', Richard Hooker, *Lawes of Ecclesiastical Polity*, I.11.2, available in multiple volumes and abridgements.

'**lead us up beyond…fill our sightless minds**', Dionysius, *Complete Works*, pp. 135–7.

'**beyond assertion and denial…by understanding**', Dionysius, *Complete Works*, p. 141.

'**our safest eloquence is silence…and reach**', Hooker, *Lawes*, I.2.3.

'**by an unaided…everything that is**', Dionysius, *Complete Works*, p. 135.

how much more deadly...enemies', Amos Funkenstein, *Theology and the Scientific Imagination* (Princeton University Press, 1986), p. 8.

'the doctrine of the Trinity...for the sake of life', Catherine LaCugna, *God For Us. The Trinity and Christian Life* (HarperCollins, 1993), p. 1.

'we become by grace what God is by nature', Athanasius, *On the Incarnation*, 54.3, in *Nicene and Post-Nicene Fathers*, Second Series, vol. 4, edited by Philip Schaff and Henry Wace (Peabody: Hendrickson, 2004), p. 65.